science for a changing world

Prepared in cooperation with Western Geographic Science Center, Menlo Park, California and University of Nevada, Reno, Nevada

Ecology of Greater Sage-Grouse in the Bi-State Planning Area Final Report, September 2007

By Michael L. Casazza, Cory T. Overton, Melissa A. Farinha, Alicia Torregrosa, Joseph P. Fleskes, Michael R. Miller, James S. Sedinger, and Eric Kolada·

Open File Report 2009–1113

U.S. Department of the Interior
U.S. Geological Survey

U.S. Department of the Interior
KEN SALAZAR, Secretary

U.S. Geological Survey
Suzette M. Kimball, Acting Director

U.S. Geological Survey, Reston, Virginia: 2009

For more information on the USGS—the Federal source for science about the Earth, its natural and living resources, natural hazards, and the environment, visit http://www.usgs.gov or call 1-888-ASK-USGS.

For an overview of USGS information products, including maps, imagery, and publications, visit *http://www.usgs.gov/pubprod*

To order this and other USGS information products, visit *http://store.usgs.gov*

Suggested citation:
Casazza, M.L., Overton, C.T., Farinha, M.A., Torregrosa, Alicia, Fleskes, J.P., Miller, M.R., Sedinger, J.S., and Kolada, Eric, 2009, Ecology of greater sage-grouse in the Bi-State Planning Area Final Report, September 2007: U.S. Geological Survey Open-File Report 2009-1113, 50 p.

Contents

Figures

Tables

Ecology of Greater Sage-Grouse in the Bi-State Planning Area Final Report, September 2007

By Michael L. Casazza, Cory T. Overton, Melissa A. Farinha, Alicia Torregrosa, Joseph P. Fleskes, Michael R. Miller, James S. Sedinger, and Eric Kolada·

Executive Summary

Conservation efforts for greater sage-grouse (*Centrocercus urophasianus*), hereafter sage-grouse, are underway across the range of this species. Over 70 local working groups have been established and are implementing on-the-ground sage-grouse oriented conservation projects. Early on in this process, the California Department of Fish and Game (CDFG) recognized the need to join in these efforts and received funding from the U.S. Fish and Wildlife Service (USFWS) under the Candidate Species Conservation Program to help develop a species conservation plan for sage-grouse in the Mono County area. This conservation plan covers portions of Alpine, Mono, and Inyo counties in California and Douglas, Esmeralda, Lyon, and Mineral counties in Nevada. A concurrent effort underway through the Nevada Governor's Sage-grouse Conservation Team established Local Area Working Groups across Nevada and eastern California. The Mono County populations of sage-grouse were encompassed by the Bi-State Local Planning Area, which was comprised of six population management units (PMUs). The state agencies from California (CDFG) and Nevada (Nevada Department of Wildlife; NDOW) responsible for the management of sage-grouse agreed to utilize the process that had begun with the Nevada Governor's Team in order to develop local plans for conservation planning and implementation.

Resources from the USFWS were applied to several objectives in support of the development of the Bi-State Local Area Sage-grouse Conservation Plan through a grant to the U.S. Geological Survey (USGS). Objectives included: (1) participate in the development of the Bi-State Conservation Plan, (2) compile and synthesize existing sage-grouse data, (3) document seasonal movements of sage-grouse, (4) identify habitats critical to sage-grouse, (5) determine survival rates and identify causal factors of mortality, (6) determine nest success and brood success of sage-grouse, and (7) identify sage-grouse lek sites. Progress reports completed in 2004 and 2005 addressed each of the specific objectives and this final report focuses on the biological information gathered in support of local conservation efforts.

Participation in the development of the Bi-State Local Area Conservation Plan was accomplished on multiple scales. Beginning in the fall of 2002, USGS personnel began participating in meetings of local stakeholders involved in the development of a sage-grouse conservation plan for the Bi-State planning area. This included attendance at numerous local PMU group meetings and field trips as well as participating on the technical advisory committee (TAC) for the Bi-State group. Whenever appropriate, ongoing results and findings regarding sage-grouse ecology in the local area were incorporated into these working group meetings. In addition, the USGS partnered with CDFG to help reorganize one of the local PMU groups (South Mono) and edited that portion of the Bi-State plan. The USGS also worked closely with CDFG to draft a description of the state of knowledge for sage-grouse genetic information for inclusion in the Bi-State Conservation Plan. The first edition of the Bi-State Conservation Plan for Greater Sage-Grouse was completed in June 2004 (Bi-State Sage-grouse Conservation Team 2004).

This report is organized primarily by PMU to facilitate the incorporation of these research findings into the individual PMU plans that compose the Bi-State plan. Information presented in this report was derived from over 7,000 radio-telemetry locations obtained on 145 individual sage-grouse during a three year period (2003-2005). In addition, we collected detailed vegetation measurements at over 590 habitat sampling plots within the study area including canopy cover, shrubs, forbs, and grasses diversity. Vegetation data collection focused on sage-grouse nests, and brood-use areas. Additionally we collected data at random sites to examine sage-grouse habitat relationships within the study area. The majority of the fieldwork was conducted within Mono County, California, although many of the radio-marked birds moved freely between various state and county jurisdictional boundaries. We radio-marked birds in four of the six Bi-State PMUs (Desert Creek/Fales, Bodie Hills, South Mono, and White Mountains), and only in one area did radio-marked birds cross PMU boundaries. Birds marked in the Bodie Hills PMU were often found in the Mt. Grant PMU as the border between these two PMUs was decided primarily for jurisdictional reasons to facilitate planning efforts and was not entirely based on specific grouse populations. Based on initial findings obtained through radio-tracking, additional information regarding the interactions between sage-grouse in the Bodie Hills and the Mt. Grant PMU is warranted.

We provided all of the sage-grouse location and movement data in both hard copy and digital format to each PMU team in order to facilitate use of these data for future sage-grouse conservation planning and project implementation. Home range sizes for sage-grouse differed by capture site and sex, with the largest home ranges in Bodie Hills PMU and some of the smaller home ranges occurring in the Desert Creek/Fales PMU and the Parker Creek area within the South Mono PMU region. The size of home ranges of hens with broods was consistent across study areas and tended to be smaller than that of most males and hens without broods. Nest survival rates were consistent between years, averaging approximately 40% from 2003 to 2005, while the average annual reproductive success (i.e. probability of a hen hatching at least one egg) was 50%. Long Valley (34%) and Fales (44%) had the lowest annual reproductive success, while the Bodie Hills and Desert Creek areas were close to 60%. Clutch size was consistent, with an average of 6.5 eggs/nest.

Mortality events were intermittent during the study with the majority occurring throughout the breeding and summer/fall seasons. The direct cause of mortality was determined as accurately as possible. Avian, mammalian, and unknown predation types occurred in similar proportion; approximately 30% each. Approximately 4% of mortalities were attributed to West Nile Virus, all of which occurred in 2004 and 2005. Common avian predators on adult sage-grouse included great horned owls (*Bubo virginianus*) and golden eagles (*Aquila chrysaetos*), while common ravens (*Corvus corax*) were documented nest predators. Mammalian predators on adult grouse included coyotes (*Canis latrans*) and bobcats (*Felis rufus*), while badgers (*Taxidea taxus*) and coyotes were documented depredators of sage-grouse nests.

Shrub cover was greater at nest sites than at random sites close to the nest (50-200m). Sage height was also generally higher at nest sites than at nearby or random sites within the study area. Vegetation at nests in the Fales region of the Desert Creek/Fales PMU had the highest percent shrub canopy cover (56.8%).

Ownership and land management responsibilities for habitats utilized by grouse varied among PMUs. Grouse were found primarily on US Forest Service (USFS) lands in the Desert Creek/Fales and White Mountains PMUs, Bureau of Land Management (BLM) lands in the Bodie Hills PMU, and Los Angeles Department of Water and Power (LADWP) lands in the South Mono PMU. Private lands provided a significant proportion of the habitat use points in the Bodie Hills, Desert Creek/Fales, and to a lesser extent the South Mono PMU.

Sage-grouse conservation in the Bi-State area is dependant on the success of the local PMU groups. These groups rely on all of the participants involved in the local conservation efforts to provide the expertise, energy, and conservation ethic necessary to implement sound conservation practices for sage-grouse. All PMUs of the Bi-State plan share a common thread. They all recognize the need for sound scientific information on which the planning and implementation of conservation efforts for sage-grouse must be based. This report provides a baseline of information for conservation of sage-grouse in the Bi-State Planning Area.

Acknowledgements

The Bi-State Local Area Sage-grouse Conservation Team provided insight, energy, and a sense of purpose towards the collection and synthesis of these data. The CDFG provided a significant portion of the funding for this project. Daniel "Sam" Blankenship initiated much of the project planning for CDFG and had the foresight to collaborate with the state of Nevada for this conservation effort. Denyse Racine of CDFG wrote the original grant to the USFWS and helped initiate the project. Scott Gardner of CDFG assisted with planning, fieldwork, and logistics, and provided an intrinsic knowledge of grouse. Local expertise regarding sage-grouse capture, vegetation sampling, and project logistics was provided by Terry Russi, Steve Nelson, Joy Fatooh, and Anne Halford from the BLM as well as Tim Taylor, Alisa Ellsworth, and Al Lapp from CDFG. Debbie House and Dale Schmidt from LADWP helped secure access to LADWP properties, provided meeting space for local PMU meetings, and provided local insight into land management. Richard Perloff and Gary Milano from the Inyo National Forest were instrumental in accomplishing much of the fieldwork in the White Mountains and vegetation data collection for Long Valley. Their project support for Sarah Alofsin, a diligent USFS field technician, helped immensely to augment the data collection efforts in the White Mountains. Mike Lawrence and Leanne Murphy from the Humboldt/Toiyabe National Forest assisted with project logistics. Laurie Sada and Kevin Kritz from the USFWS provided insight into the conservation planning process and financial support through a grant from the USFWS/USGS Science Support Program. Jack Connelly, Idaho Department of Fish and Game and Tony Apa, Colorado Division of Wildlife, provided helpful comments on the initial study plan. Walt Mandeville and

Shawn Espinosa of NDOW provided insight into sage-grouse biology in Nevada. The dedicated field crews demonstrated a true concern for the conservation of sage-grouse in this region and included; Roberta Montana, Jeffrey Felland, Kristie Nelson, Blake Barbaree, Heather Gates, Matthew Toomey, Kim Gagnon, Gordon Watts Jr., Tim Skousen, Donna Young, Roger Ratcliff, Cynthia Drake. The staff at the Dixon Field Station of the Western Ecological Research Center (WERC) of USGS contributed greatly to the completion of this project. Pamela Gore provided administrative support while William Perry provided GIS and website expertise. We thank Dick Haldeman and Leann Fields of Quail Unlimited for providing financial and logistical support. Karen Phillips, Tom Suchanek, Roger Hothem and Josh Ackerman from WERC provided helpful reviews. A grant from the Science Impact Program of the USGS provided additional funding.

Conservation Planning

The primary objective of this project was to facilitate the conservation planning effort underway through the Nevada Governor's Sage-grouse Conservation Team, and more specifically help develop the Local Area Sage-grouse Conservation Plan for the Bi-State Local Planning Area (Figure 1). The plans developed through the Nevada Governor's Sage-grouse Conservation Team are consensus-built conservation plans produced by local working groups, including federal, state, and local regulatory and land-management agencies, non-governmental organizations, ranchers, private landowners, and Native American tribes.

The Bi-State Local Area Conservation Planning Group encompasses six sage-grouse population management units (PMUs) along the California/Nevada border including areas in Mono, Inyo, and Alpine counties in California and Lyon and Mineral counties in Nevada. The six PMUs include Desert Creek/Fales, Bodie Hills, South Mono, Pine Nut, White Mountains, and Mt. Grant. Local population risk assessments and conservation strategies have been developed in each PMU and a "First Edition" of the Bi-State Conservation Plan was submitted in June 2004 (Bi-State Sage-grouse Conservation Team 2004).

Two documents provide insight into the status of sage-grouse from a range-wide perspective. A recent finding by the USFWS (Deibert 2005) that listing of the sage-grouse was not warranted under the Endangered Species Act was based in part on the fact that numerous local conservation plans were in various stages of development. The second document was a range-wide assessment (Connelly et al. 2004) which summarized the current state of knowledge regarding sage-grouse and sagebrush habitats across the West. A petition to implement an emergency listing of the Mono Basin sage-grouse as endangered was first submitted in December of 2001. The 90-day finding, published in the Federal Register on December 26, 2002, indicated that the information presented in the petition was not substantial, and emergency listing thus not warranted. Since that initial finding, a subsequent study of sage-grouse genetics indicated that the grouse in Mono, Lyon, and Mineral counties appear to be genetically unique and may warrant special attention (Oyler-McCance et al. 2005). Subsequent to these genetic findings, a new petition was filed in November of 2005 to list the Mono Basin sage-grouse under the Endangered Species Act.

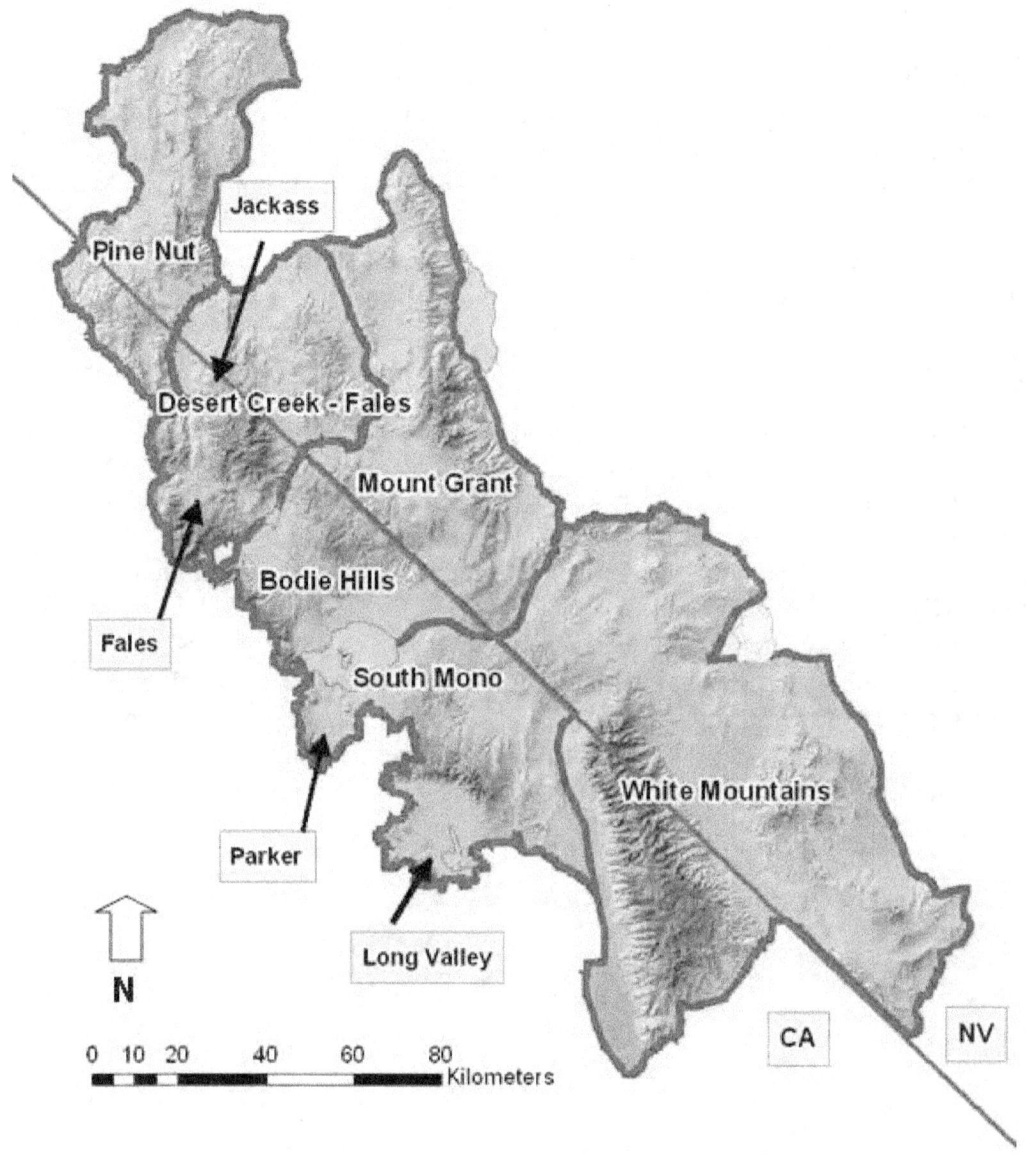

Figure 1. The Bi-State Planning Area with Population Management Unit boundaries (green).

USGS personnel have participated in the conservation planning process over the past several years through a variety of means. Our scientists attended both Bi-State and local PMU planning meetings and presented scientific findings and results from ongoing local field studies of sage-grouse ecology to these local working groups. We partnered with CDFG to facilitate the "South Mono PMU Group" and have provided technical assistance as needed to other local PMU groups.

Beginning in spring 2003, we coordinated with local, state, and federal agencies and conservation and landowner groups to initiate field studies designed to fufill information needs for sage-grouse conservation planning in the region. We collected data using a variety of research tools including radio-telemetry, standardized vegetation sampling, and direct observation. The telemetry dataset (over 7,000 individual observations) along with the corresponding metadata, has been incorporated into the BIOS database maintained by CDFG. The majority of the field work occurred within Mono County, California. This report summarizes the results from this work in an effort to provide a sound scientific dataset in support of the ongoing local conservation efforts.

Field Studies

We radio-marked and tracked 145 individual sage-grouse from March 2003 through October 2005 at six different study sites (Table 1). Birds were captured in close proximity to leks in the spring and at various concentration areas during the fall using nighttime spotlighting techniques and dip nets (Wakkinen et al. 1992, Giesen et al. 1982). We used 26g Advanced Telemetry Systems, Inc (Isanti, MN) necklace mounted transmitters, Model A4060 (Riley and Fistler 1992, Sveum et al. 1998). Our goal was to locate each bird at least two times each week, while monitoring nesting or brood rearing hens at least four times each week. We attempted to maintain at least 50 active transmitters at any one time during the study. We tracked approximately 40 birds during 2003, 70 birds during 2004, and 60 birds during 2005 (Table 2). Sage-grouse were radio-marked in Mono County, CA, but many were subsequently located in several areas within Nevada including the Mt. Grant PMU and the Desert Creek portion of the Desert Creek/Fales PMU (Figure 2).

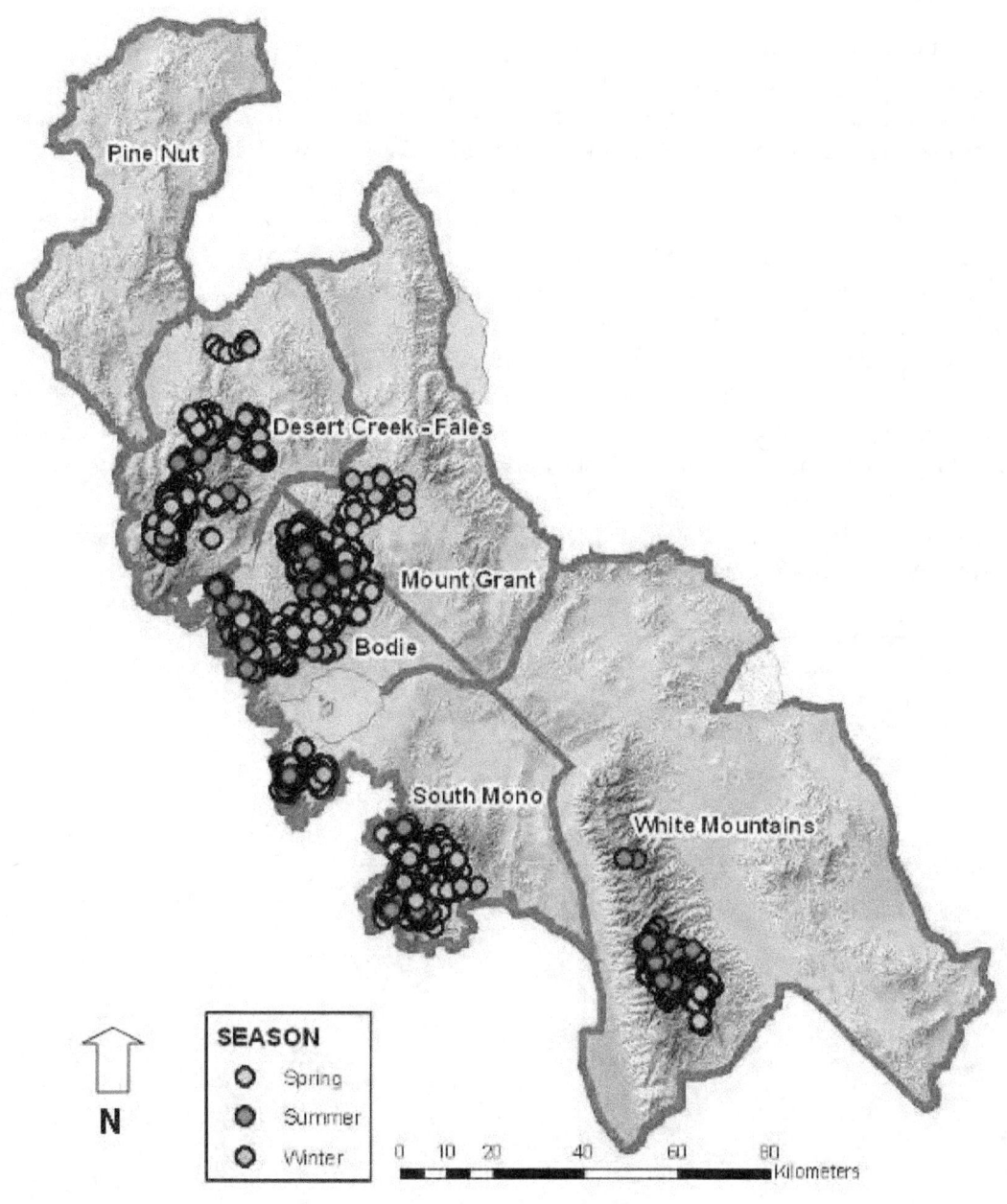

Figure 2. Locations of radio-marked sage-grouse March 2003 – October 2005 in the Bi-State Planning Area.

Bird Movements:

Annual home ranges were calculated using fixed kernel analysis for all individuals with more than 30 locations throughout the year and no less than 7 locations in either the spring or summer season. The Spring season lasted from April through June, Summer included July-October, Fall/Winter (hereafter Winter) was November to March. Home range sizes for radio-marked grouse differed between study areas, with 2 male birds in the Bodie Hills having the largest home ranges (> 17,000 hectares) and a male grouse in the Fales area having the smallest home range (only 608 hectares) (Table 3). We examined differences in home range size for males, females with broods, and females without broods (Figure 3). Males tended to have the largest home ranges, followed by females without broods, and then females with broods. We used seasonal home range polygons to describe individual bird movements within each PMU. Migratory behavior as defined in "Guidelines to manage sage-grouse populations and their habitat" (Connelly et al. 2000; greater than 10km between seasonal use areas) was uncommon in most study areas. Some of the bird movements within the Bodie Hills, Desert Creek/Fales, and White Mountains PMU would be classified as migratory, but the majority of radio-marked individuals did not move as far as 10 km between seasonal use areas.

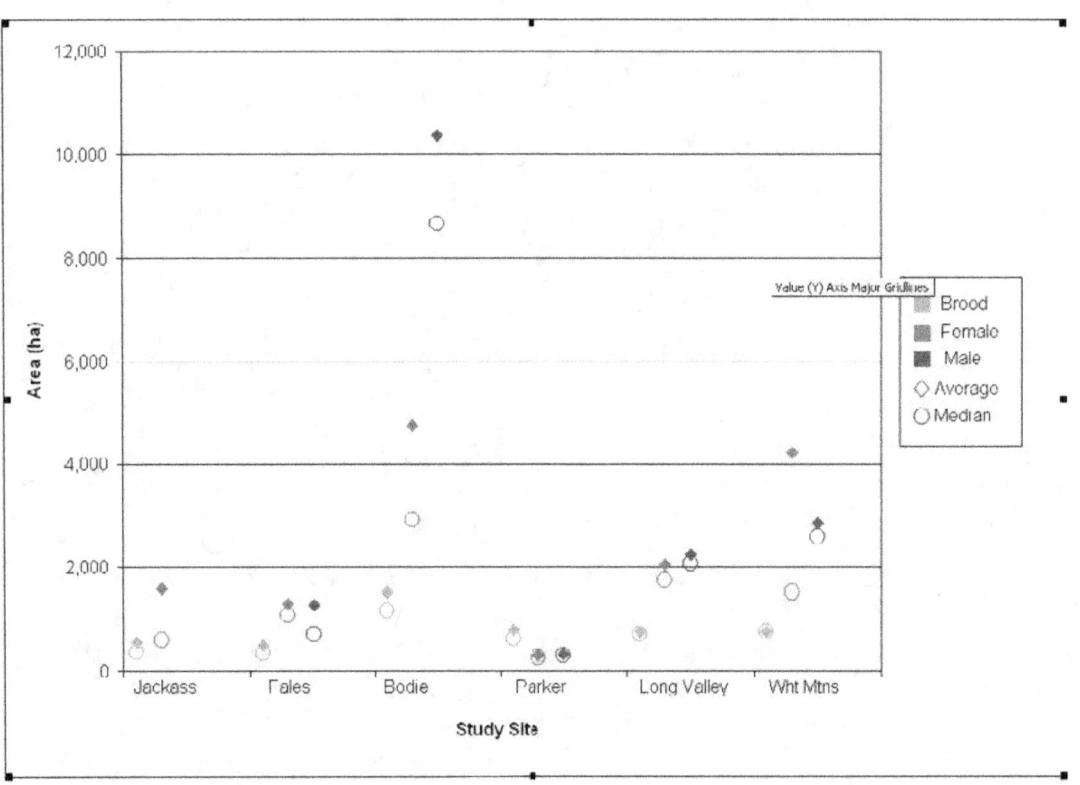

Figure 3. Average and median spring/summer home range sizes for males (blue), females without successful broods (red), and females with successful broods (green) within each study area. Home ranges calculated for each sage-grouse with >30 telemetry locations obtained between April and October, with no less than 7 telemetry locations in either Spring (April-June) or Summer (July-October) seasons.

Land ownership was highly variable between PMUs (Figure 4). Sage-grouse in the White Mountains and the Desert Creek/Fales PMU were primarily located on USFS land, while the BLM lands were a significant portion of the habitat use in the Bodie Hills PMU. We found sage-grouse in the South Mono PMU concentrating their habitat use on a mix of LADWP, BLM, and USFS lands. Private lands were not used extensively in any of the PMUs, although the Bodie Hills and the Desert Creek/Fales area PMUs experienced some private land use.

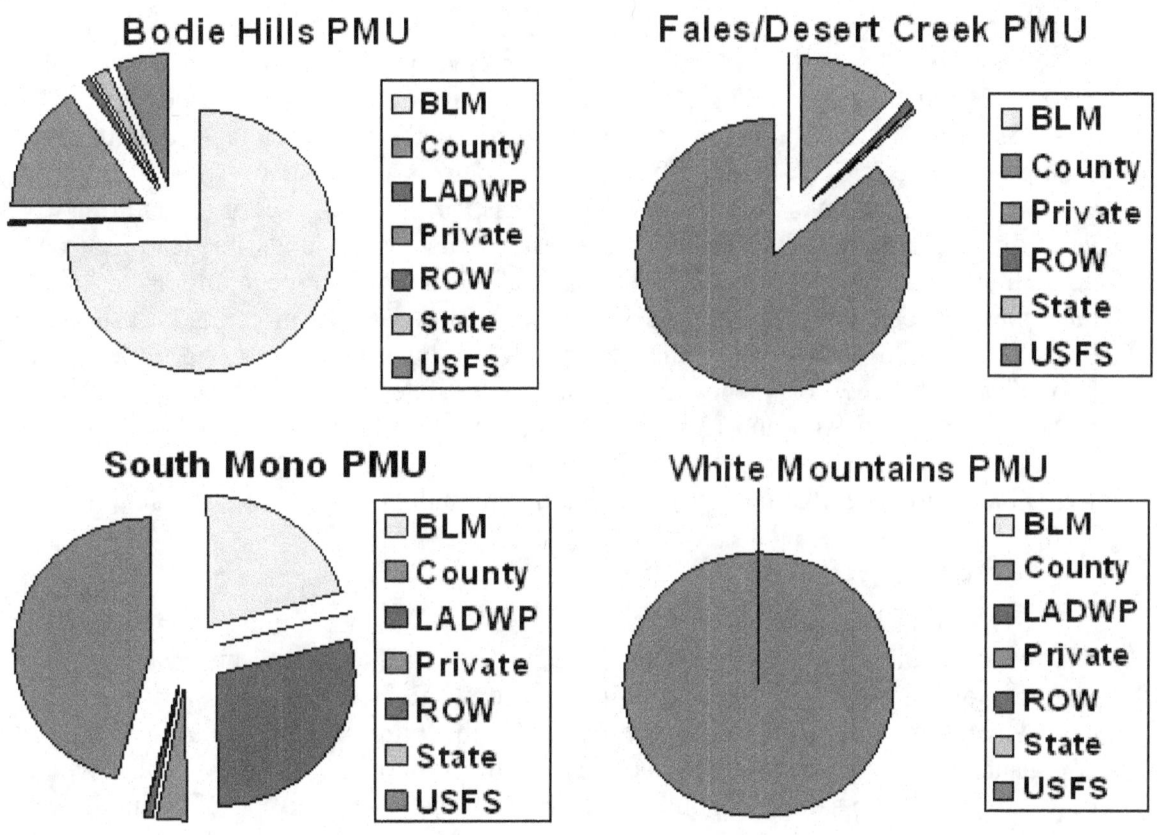

† ROW – Right of Way (various ownership)

Figure 4. Land ownership of radio-marked sage-grouse home ranges in each PMU†.

Mortality Factors:

Transmitters were equipped with mortality sensors which doubled the transmitter pulse rate after 8 hours of non-movement. We attempted to recover all sage-grouse remains upon mortality signal detection in order to identify the direct cause of mortality. We tabulated causes of mortality for radio-marked sage-grouse in each of the study areas using all available indicators, including carcass composition, environment in which carcass found, searching the surrounding area for predator-type indicators, and consideration of length of time after radio transmitter application (Table 4). Avian predators played a significant role in mortality causes in both the Bodie Hills and the White Mountains PMU, while mammalian predators made up a higher proportion of mortalities in the South Mono PMU (Table 4). Identification of direct causes of mortality can be difficult to ascertain without visual observation of an event, especially with respect to disease outbreaks, as sick birds may be more susceptible to predation.

Nesting:

We summarized nesting data for radio-marked hens from 2003-2005 (Table 5). Nominal nest success is defined as the proportion of radio-marked birds alive through the nesting season that had a successful nest (at least 1 egg hatched; Table 6). Nominal nest success was consistent between years and ranged between 44-54% for all study sites. Clutch size was also consistent between years and averaged about 6.5 eggs/nest (Table 5). Re-nesting rates were relatively low but did contribute to nominal success rates.

Proximate causes for a successful sage-grouse nest versus an unsuccessful sage-grouse nest were difficult to quantify. Ongoing analysis as part of a graduate study will address some of the links to vegetative characteristics and nest success. In addition to vegetative features, variables such as slope, aspect, distance to landscape features (roads, powerlines, leks, etc.) are also being examined. Information on predator densities and movement patterns could also provide insight into causal factors affecting nest success. In 2005, we deployed five nest cameras at several nests, primarily in Long Valley, in a pilot effort to test their efficiency in determining nest fate. Cameras used a passive infrared triggering sensor and 15 second video clips. Nests without cameras in 2005 and all nests in 2003 and 2004 were evaluated for cause of failure using nest remains. We were able to document both avian (raven) and mammalian (coyote) nest predation.

Habitat Plots:

We conducted detailed habitat sampling measurements at multiple locations within each study area. Twenty-meter transects were used to obtain shrub canopy and composition measurements. Five equidistance points along the transect were used for concealment measurements (robel pole). Five Daubenmire frames were also placed equidistant along each transect for plant height and composition measurements. We defined a vegetation sampling point as the center of the 20-m transect. We sampled at each nest location, at random points in close proximity to nests determined by random compass bearing, and at a random distance of 50-200 meters ("dependent random"), and at random points within the study area boundaries determined using GIS ("independent random"). We collected a total of 590 habitat sampling points, including a subset of "brood" locations at which a brood was present with the radio-marked hen (Figure 5).

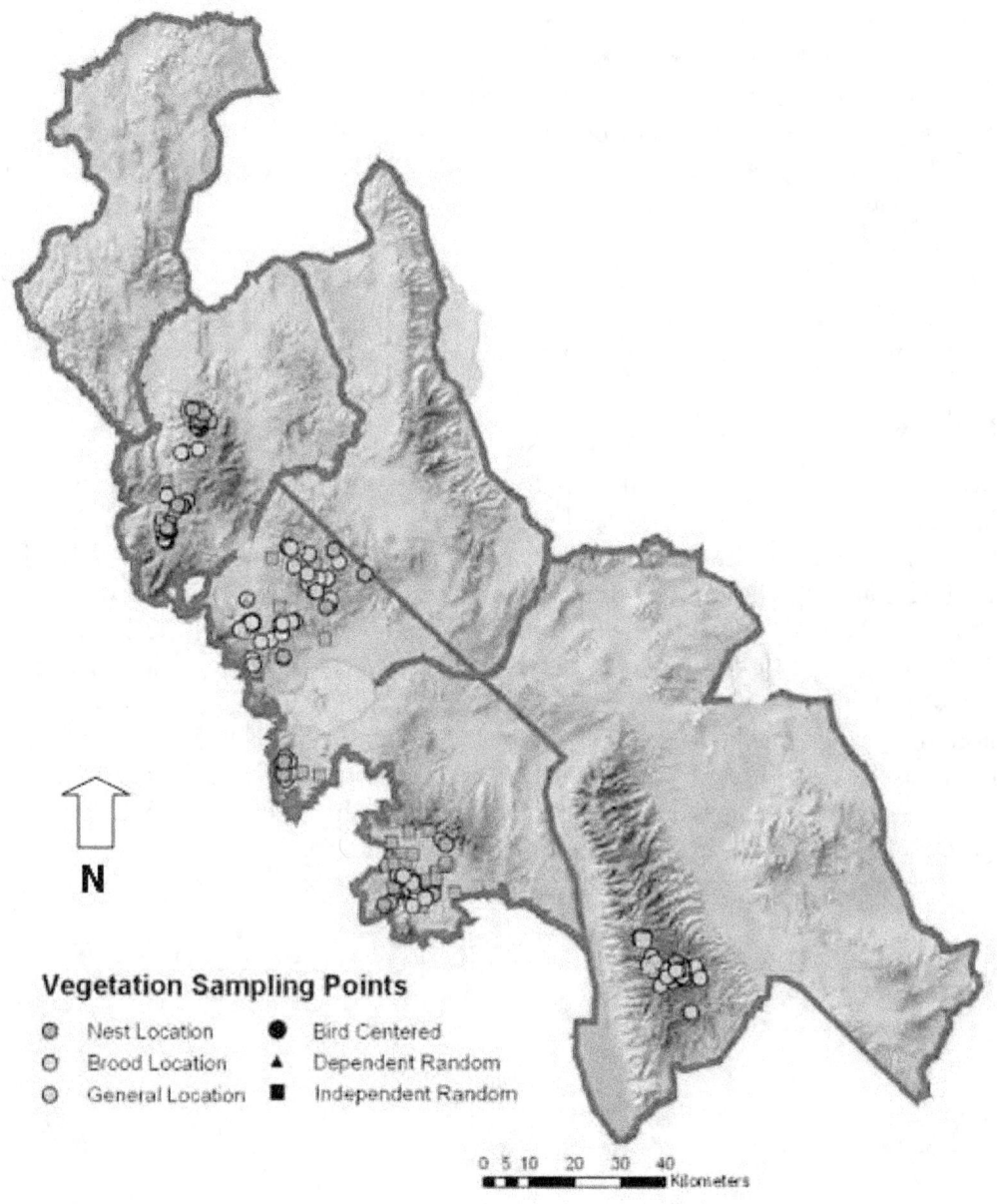

Figure 5. Vegetation sampling conducted at 590 locations within the Bi-State Planning Area between 2003 and 2005. Sampling completed at bird locations (circles) was paired with sampling done at random locations 50 to 200 meters away (triangles). We also sampled at random locations within the study area (squares). Note: Some locations not visible due to map scale.

Habitat characteristics at nest sites differed from measurements at random and dependent random points (Table 7). Canopy cover was greatest at nests in the Fales area with 56.8% cover, with dependant random and independent random points lower at 42.2% and 43.3% respectively. Sage heights along transects at nests were generally higher than sage heights at random or dependant random transects. Average sagebrush heights in the Fales study area were tallest at nest plots (64 cm), while the tallest average sagebrush among random points were found in Long Valley (67 cm). The Long Valley points included several locations that occurred primarily on the east bench near Wilfred Creek/Waterson Canyon, along the Glass Mountains and the west bench wintering area north of Little Hot Creek (Table 2). Future analysis of habitat plot data will include an investigation of the relationship between vegetative characteristics and nesting success.

Desert Creek/Fales PMU

We radio-marked and tracked 35 individual sage-grouse (10 males and 25 females within the Desert Creek/Fales PMU (Table 1). Trapping occurred during the spring adjacent to leks located at Burcham Flat, Wheeler Flat, and Jackass Spring. We obtained telemetry locations on radio-marked birds throughout the year (Figure 6). However, sample sizes in the Burcham and Wheeler areas was very low following the 2004 breeding season and no transmitters were active at the end of the study period (Table 2).

Most of the birds marked near the Jackass lek either remained in the area throughout the year or moved to the adjacent burn southeast of the lek during the spring and summer each year (Figure 6). However, during the winter of 2003-2004 and 2004-2005, several individuals moved to lower elevations near the Sweetwater Ranch area and Wiley Ditch leks and the south end of Smith Valley (Figure 6).

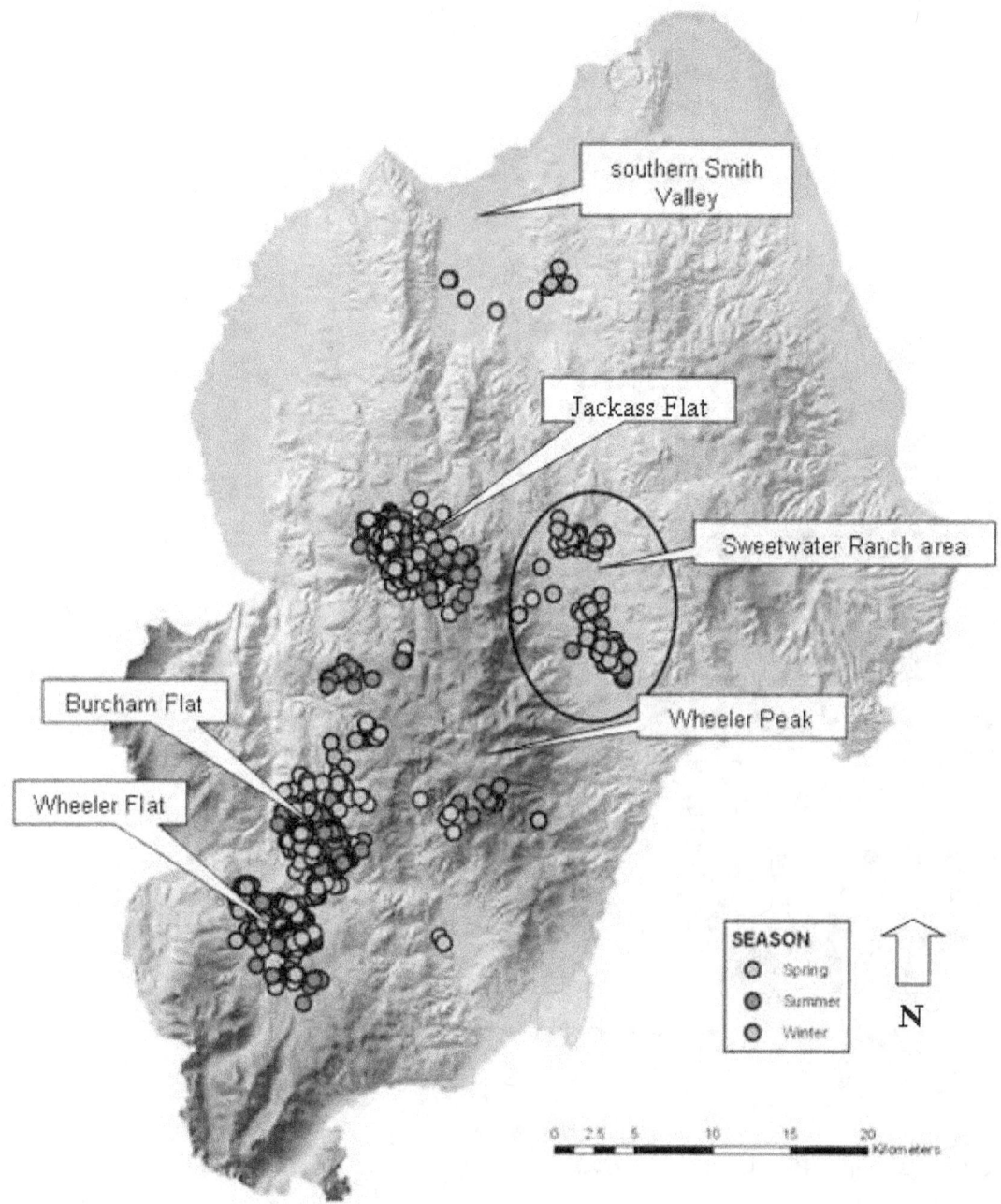

Figure 6. Radio-marked sage-grouse locations in the Desert Creek/Fales PMU March 2003 – October 2005. (Spring = April-June; Summer = July-October; Winter = November-March).

One female took her brood to the area north of Little Deep Creek during the late brood period. Most of the radio-marked birds within Burcham and Wheeler areas remained in a relatively small area near their respective leks during all seasons. Most birds from the Fales area spent the spring and summer on Wheeler Flat, west of Hwy-395 or the slopes above Burcham Flat. Sage-grouse used Burcham Flat itself mostly during the winter. A few of the male grouse moved to high elevation meadows near the top of the Sweetwater Mountains in the vicinity of Wheeler Peak, especially near Lobdell Lake. Unmarked sage-grouse were encountered in the same general locations as marked grouse (Figure 7), with several large flocks of up to 90 birds recorded in the Sweetwater Ranch area.

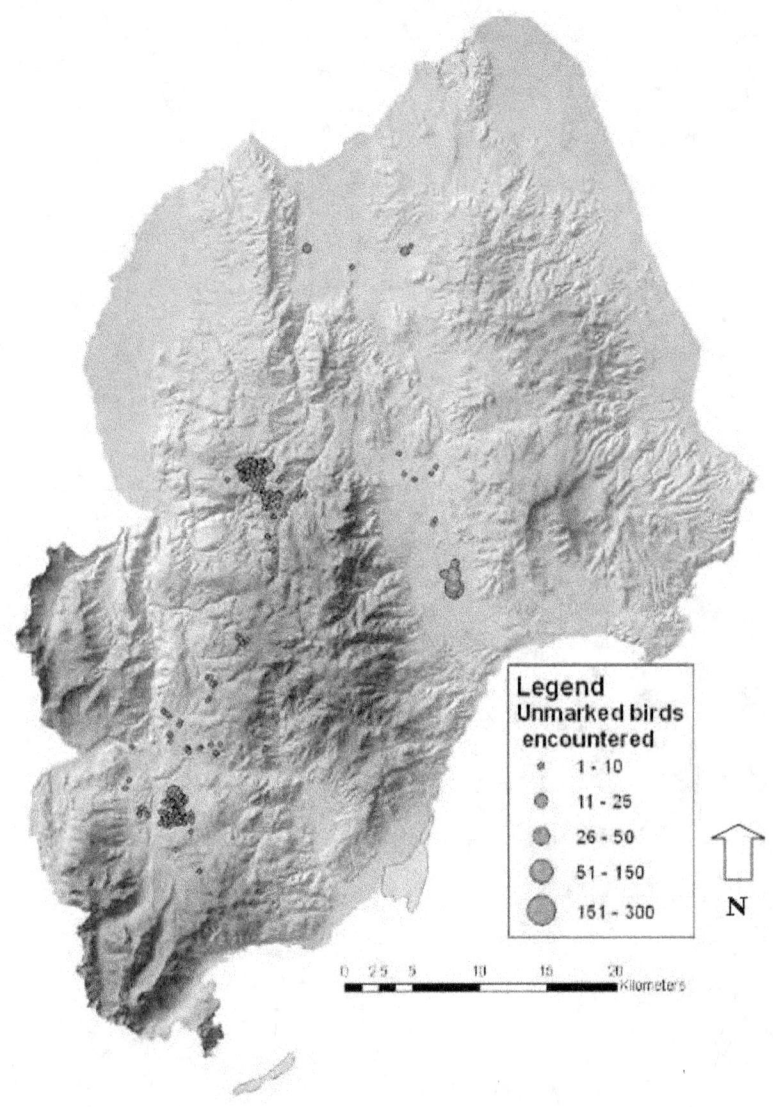

Desert Creek/Fales PMU

Figure 7. Location of unmarked sage-grouse observations obtained during field studies in the Desert Creek/Fales PMU, 2003-2005.

Nest locations for radio-marked hens in the Desert Creek/Fales PMU were in close proximity of the lek closest to their capture location (Figure 8). After hatching, radio-marked hens kept their broods fairly close to their respective nesting locations (Figure 8, 9).

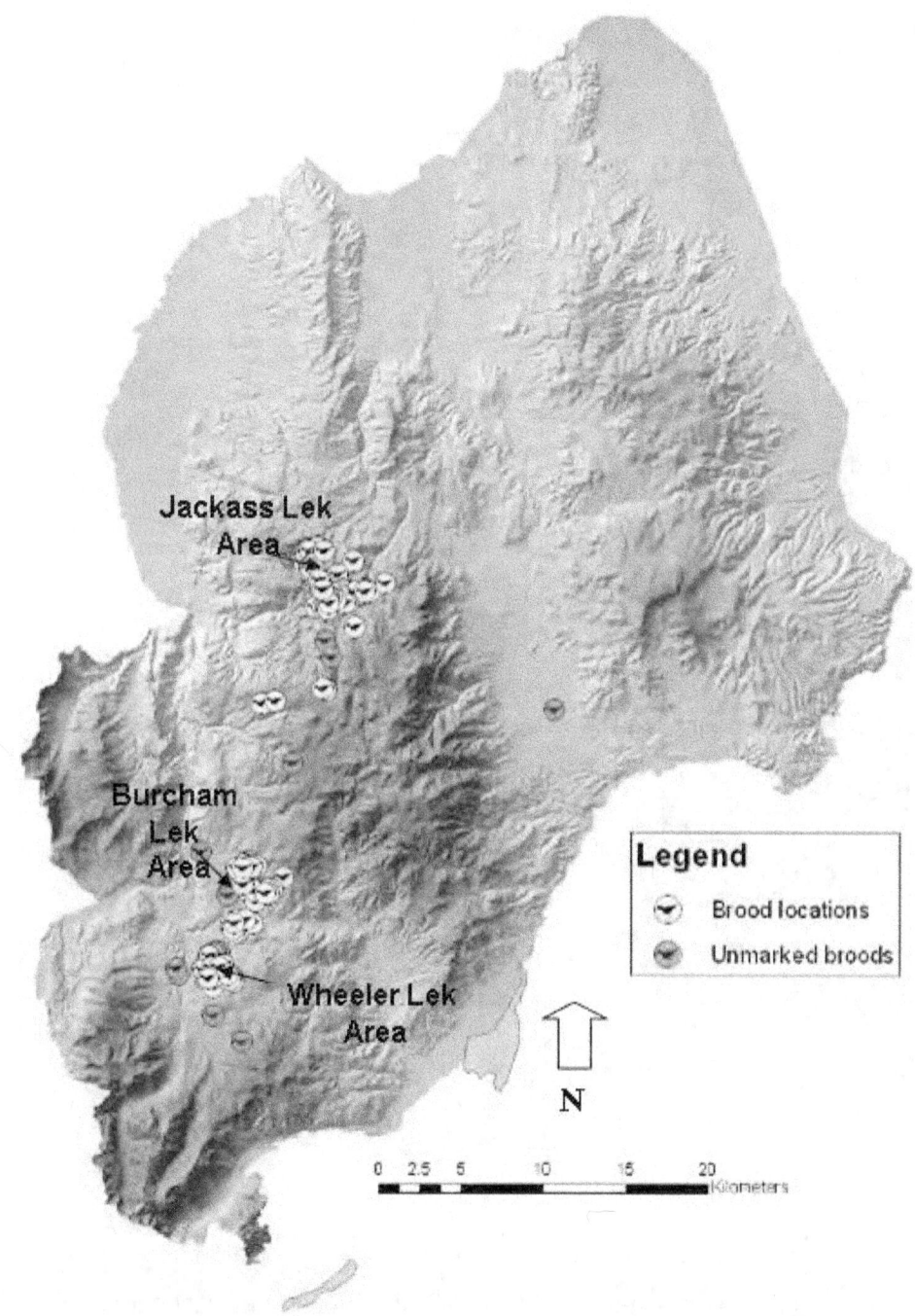

Desert Creek/Fales PMU

Figure 8. Nest locations of radio-marked sage-grouse in the Desert Creek/Fales PMU during the 2003 and 2004 nesting seasons.

The one exception to this was the aforementioned hen marked near the Jackass lek that moved her brood into an area that had recently burned and was several kilometers south of her nesting location (Figure 9). Hens typically took their broods to one or more common areas also used by other marked birds where integration of hens and broods occurred.

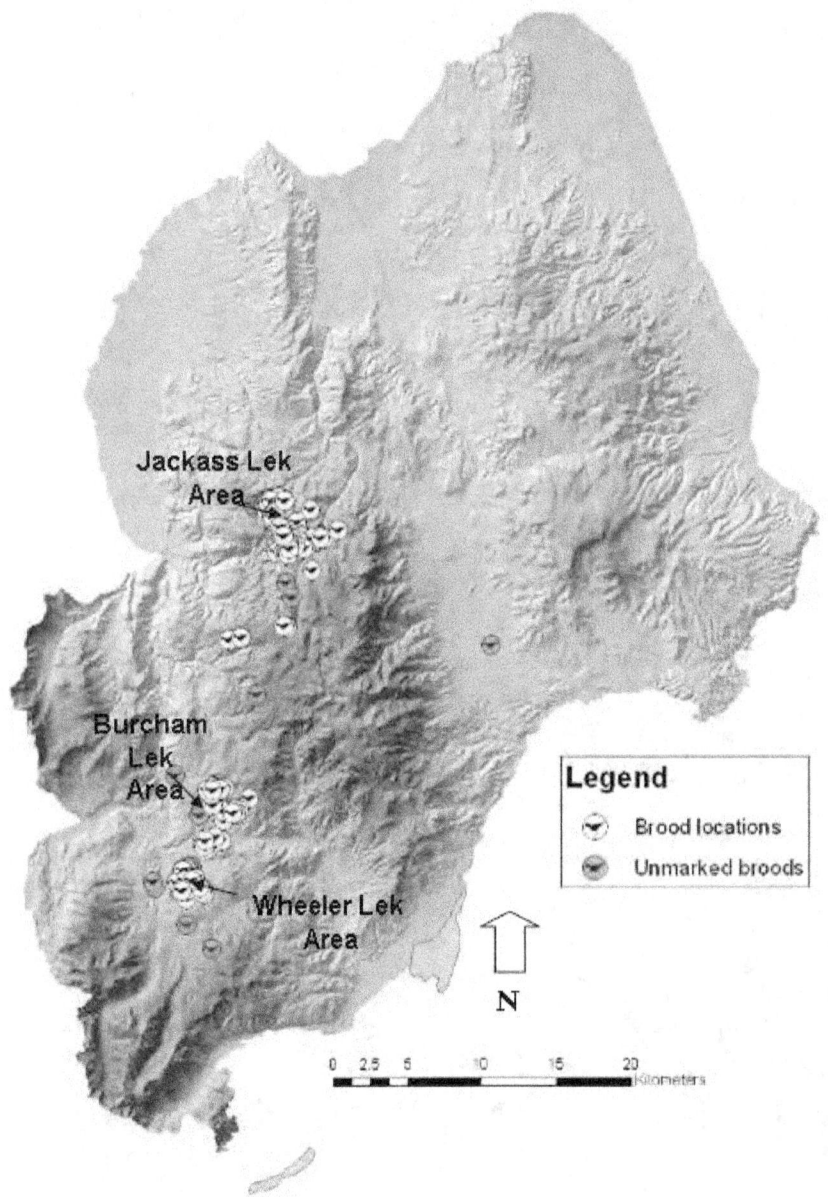

Desert Creek/Fales PMU

Figure 9. Locations of radio-marked sage-grouse hens with their broods, and opportunistically encountered unmarked broods in the Desert Creek/Fales PMU, 2003-2005.

Mortality events were located across the PMU but were centered near the lek areas near Jackass Spring and Wheeler and Burcham Flats (Figure 10).

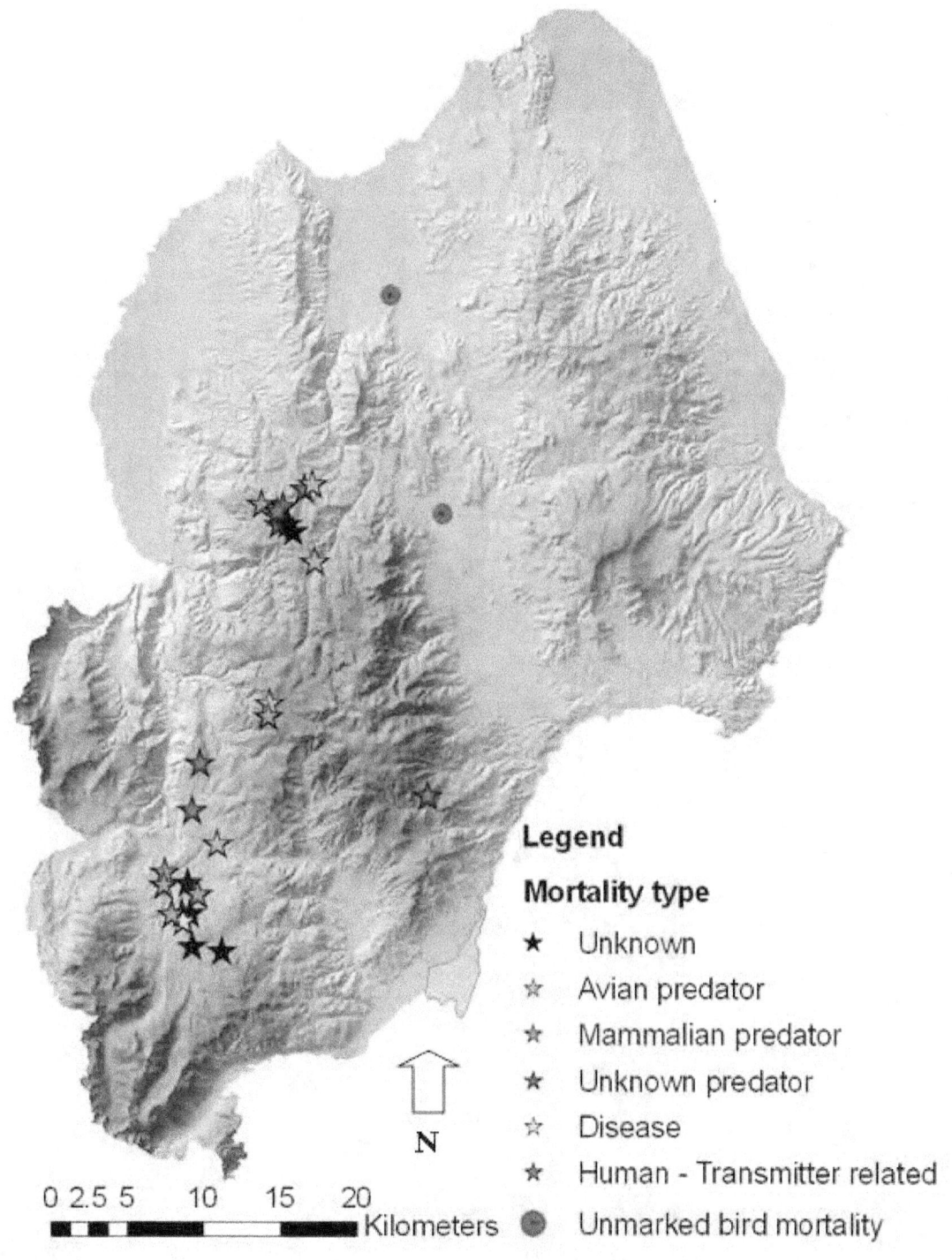

Legend

Mortality type

★   Unknown

☆   Avian predator

✩   Mammalian predator

★   Unknown predator

☆   Disease

★   Human - Transmitter related

●   Unmarked bird mortality

Desert Creek/Fales PMU

Figure 10. Location and type of sage-grouse mortality events in the Desert Creek/Fales PMU, 2003-2005.

We did not record any radio-marked bird mortalities on the lower elevation use areas in Nevada (i.e. southern Smith Valley and Sweetwater Ranch areas). Use areas did not vary widely between years or between seasons (Figure 11) except for increased use of Wheeler Peak in the summer and southern Smith Valley in the winter.

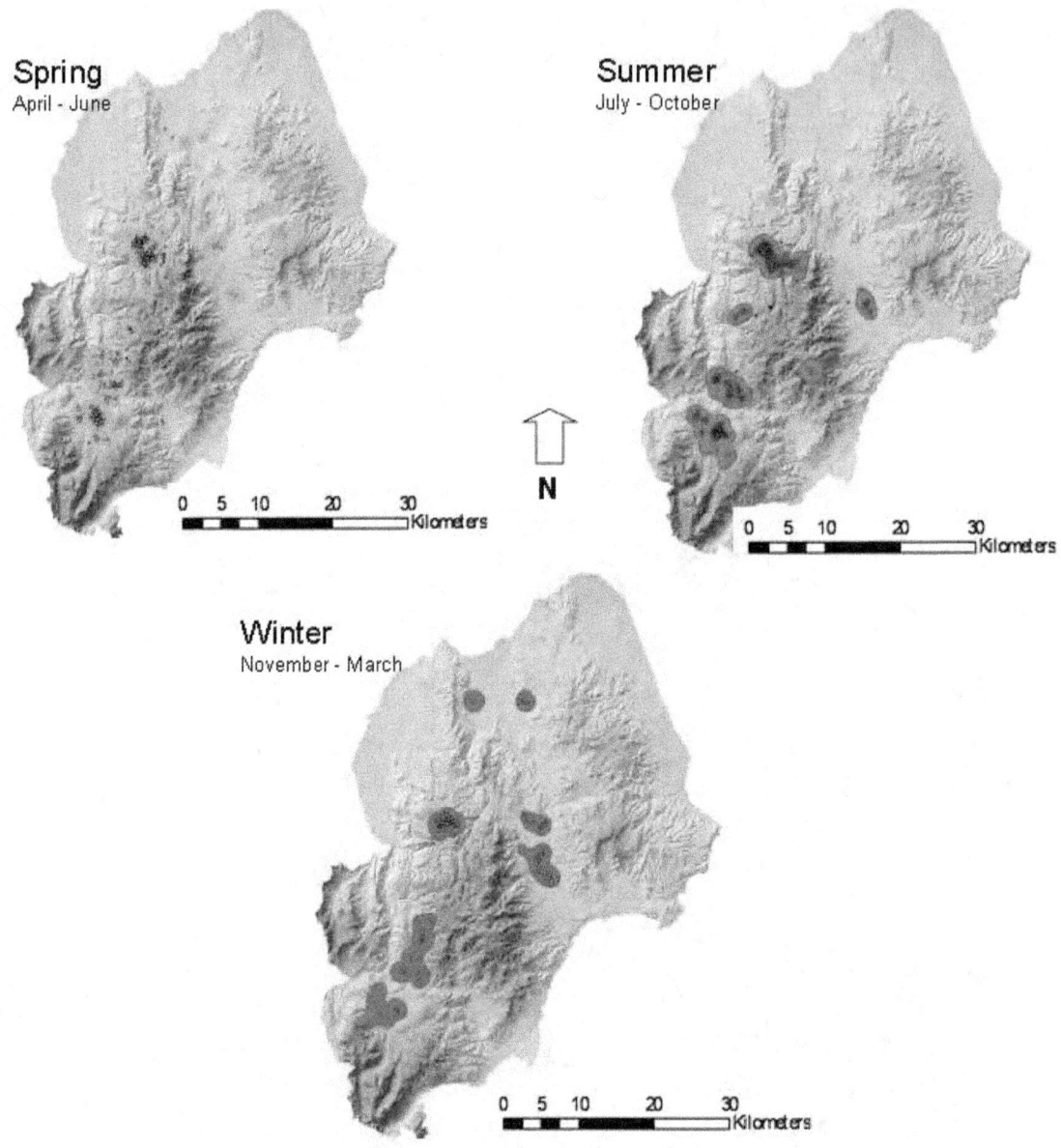

Desert Creek/Fales PMU

Figure 11. Seasonal sage-grouse use areas in the Desert Creek/Fales PMU, 2003-2005. (Spring = April-June; Summer = July-October; Winter = November-March).

Likewise, the pattern of land ownership within home ranges did not vary substantially across seasons (Figure 12). The majority of home ranges in all seasons existed on lands managed by the U.S. Forest Service Toyaibe National Forest. However, a substantial portion of home ranges in the Desert Creek/Fales PMU occurred on private lands, mostly in Burcham and Wheeler Flats.

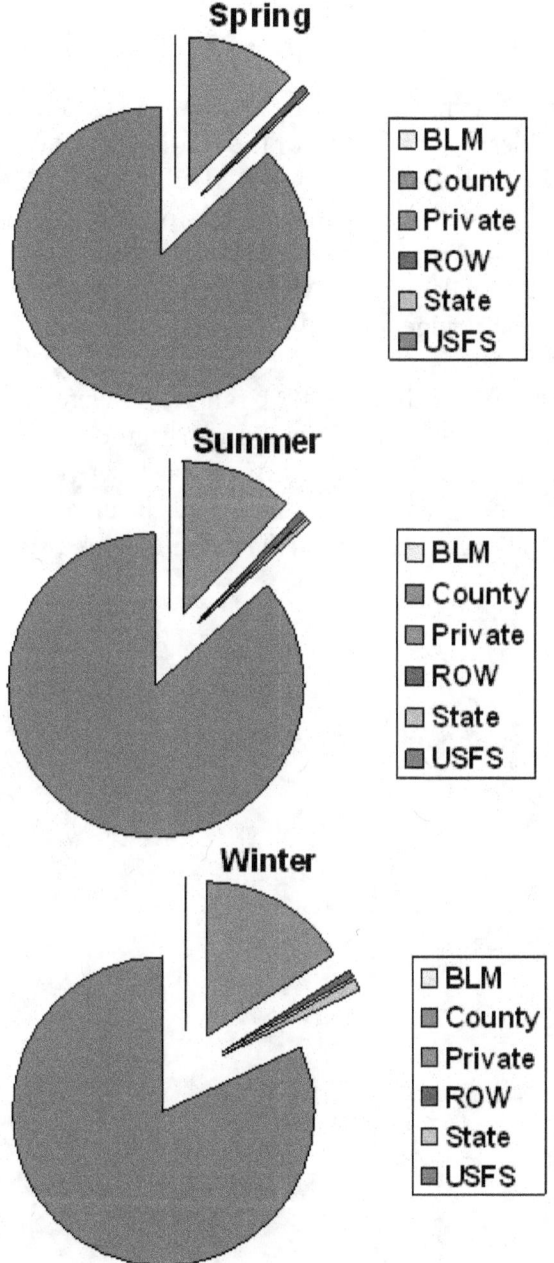

Figure 12. Land ownership within seasonal home ranges for radio-marked sage-grouse in the Desert Creek/Fales PMU.

Bodie Hills PMU/Mt. Grant PMU

We tracked 37 sage-grouse (9 males, 28 females) within the Bodie Hills PMU. Some of these marked individuals were subsequently located within the Mt. Grant PMU and therefore data for both PMUs are presented here. Birds were trapped at several locations within the Bodie Hills PMU, with most captures in the vicinity of the Dry Lakes, Big Flat, and Bridgeport Canyon areas. Radio-marked grouse were tracked beginning in the spring of 2003, and 6 transmitters (1 male, 5 female) were still active at the end of the study period (Table 2).

Sage-grouse marked in the Bodie Hills PMU had the largest and the most variable home ranges of all areas studied (Table 3). Widespread portions of the Bodie Hills PMU were used in all seasons by radio-marked grouse (Figure 13) with unmarked grouse often encountered in close proximity (Figure 14). Consistent use occurred year-round at Dry Lakes and the north and west sides of Big Flat. The most concentrated use occurred in the meadow regions, especially at Big Flat and near Paramount Mine, during the late summer; however sage brush and meadows in the Bridgeport Valley, and Green Creek drainage were also used extensively in the summer.

The China Camp and Nine Mile Ranch areas within the Mt. Grant PMU were primarily used by marked birds from Bodie Hills during the winter period (Figure 13). Marked grouse generally used the area between Mt. Biedeman and Bridgeport Canyon during winter and spring. The north and east slopes of Bodie Mountain and the area around Paramount Mine were used during the spring and summer. The Big Flat area was used mostly in the summer and winter.

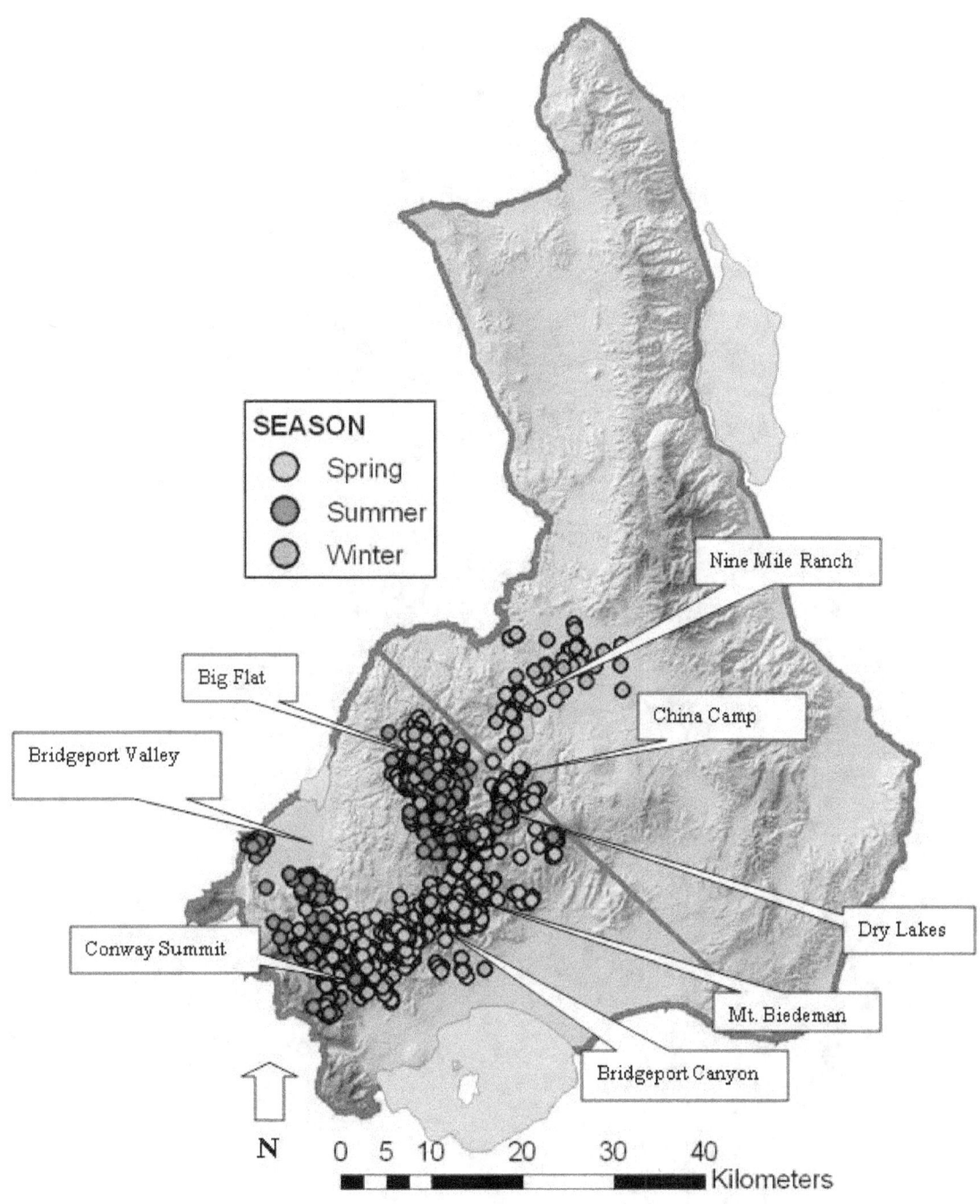

Bodie Hills and Mt. Grant PMUs

Figure 13. Radio-marked sage-grouse locations in the Bodie Hills and Mt. Grant PMUs March 2003 – October 2005. (Spring = April-June; Summer = July-October; Winter = November-March).

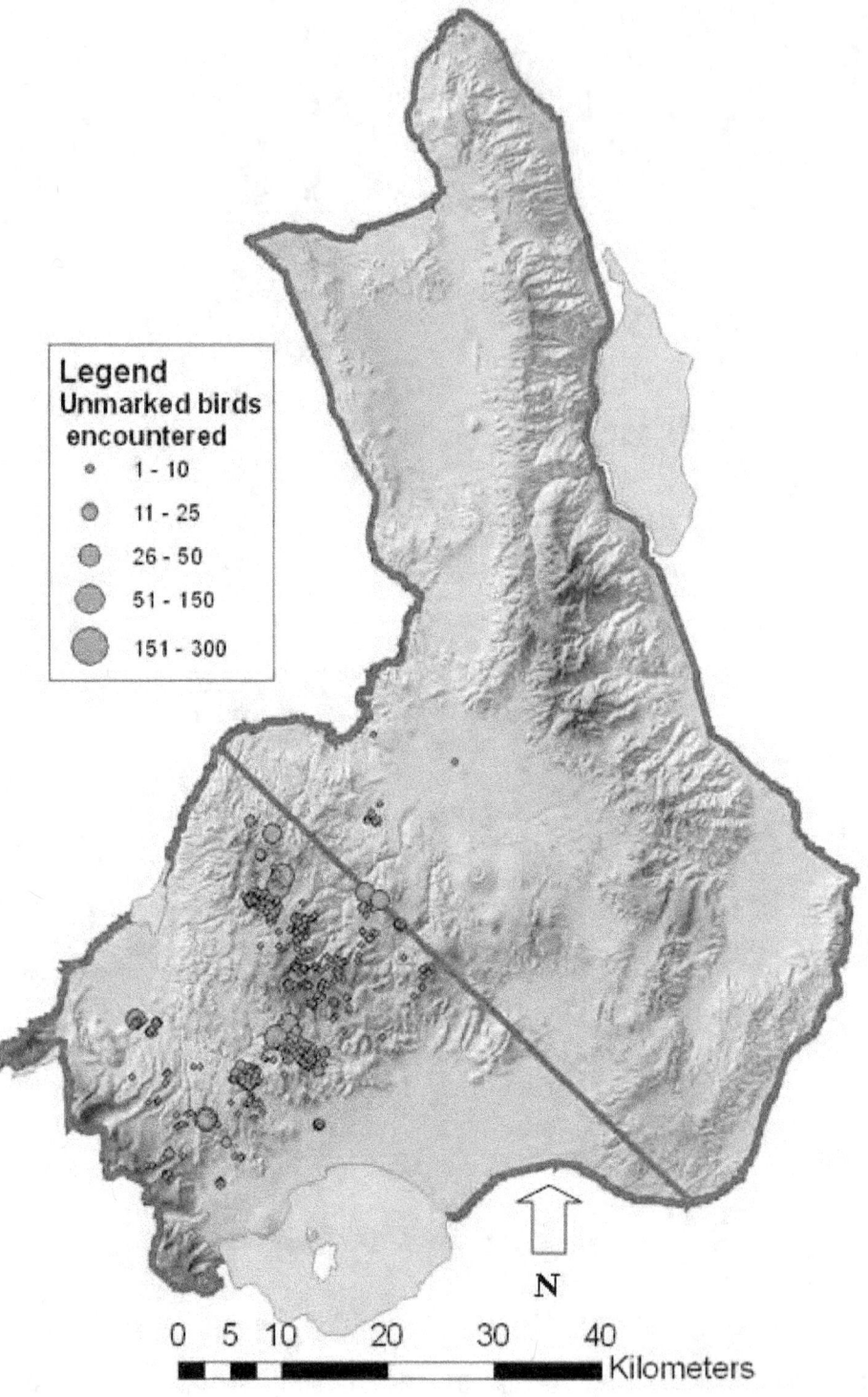

Bodie Hills and Mt. Grant PMUs

Figure 14. Location of unmarked sage-grouse observations obtained during field studies in the Bodie Hills and Mt. Grant PMUs, 2003-2005.

The radio-marked hens in the Bodie Hills PMU nested in fairly close proximity to their capture lek, with few exceptions (Figure 15). Two birds nested far from any known lek on the southern edge of the Bodie Hills overlooking Mono Lake. Overall, nests were distributed throughout the PMU. The vegetation structure associated with nests in the Bodie Hills PMU had a higher percent canopy closure and a higher non-sagebrush component (bitterbrush, *Purshia tridentata*) than in other PMUs.

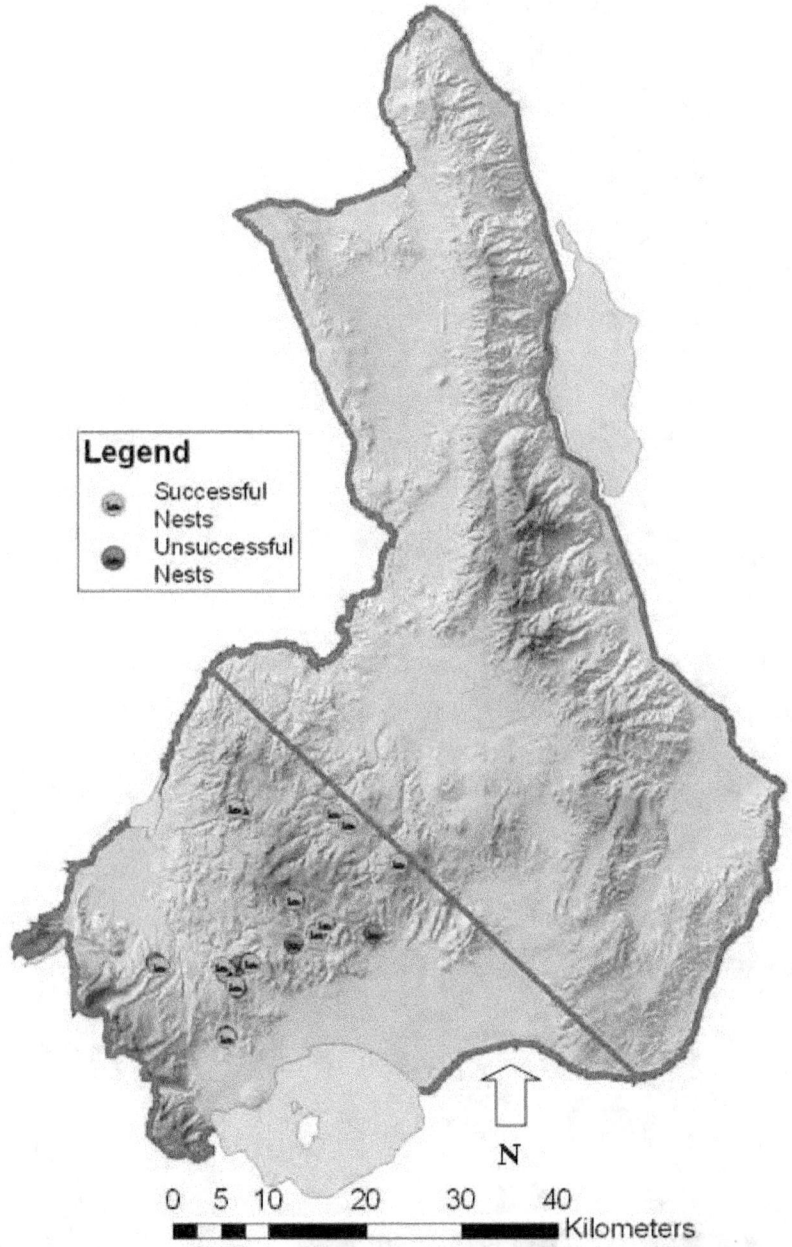

Bodie Hills and Mt. Grant PMUs

Figure 15. Nest locations for radio-marked sage-grouse in the Bodie Hills PMU, 2003-2005.

Brood locations were distributed throughout the PMU but concentrated in the area of Conway summit and the southern end of Bridgeport Valley as well as the area to the west of Mt. Biedeman (Figure 16).

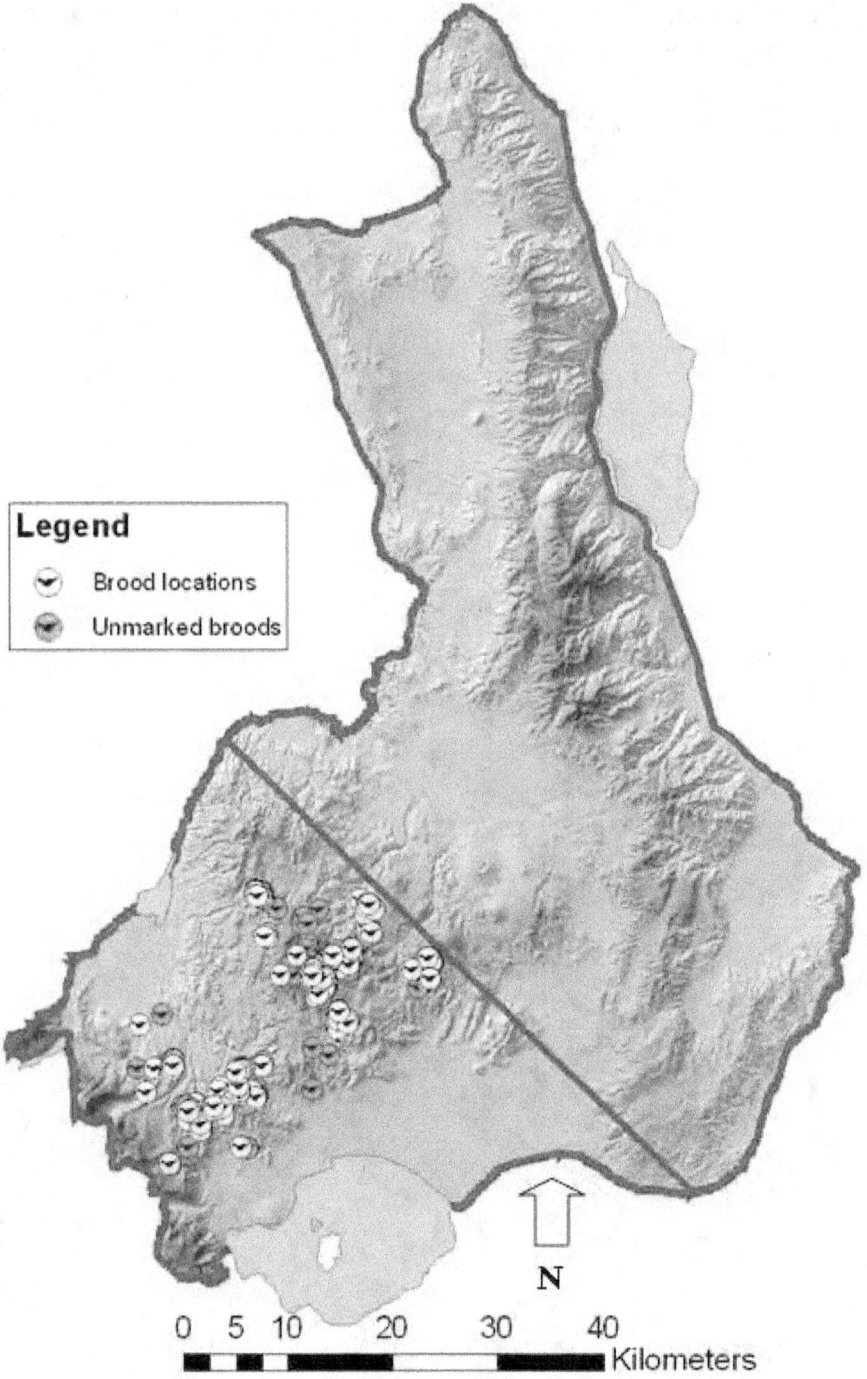

Bodie Hills and Mt. Grant PMUs

Figure 16. Locations of radio-marked sage-grouse hens with their broods, and opportunistically encountered unmarked broods in the Bodie Hills PMU, 2003-2005.

We found dead radio-marked sage-grouse at numerous sites across the Bodie Hills PMU while no mortality of radio-marked birds occurred in the Mt. Grant PMU (Figure 17). West Nile virus was detected most often (three sage-grouse infected) within the Bodie Hills PMU (Table 4).

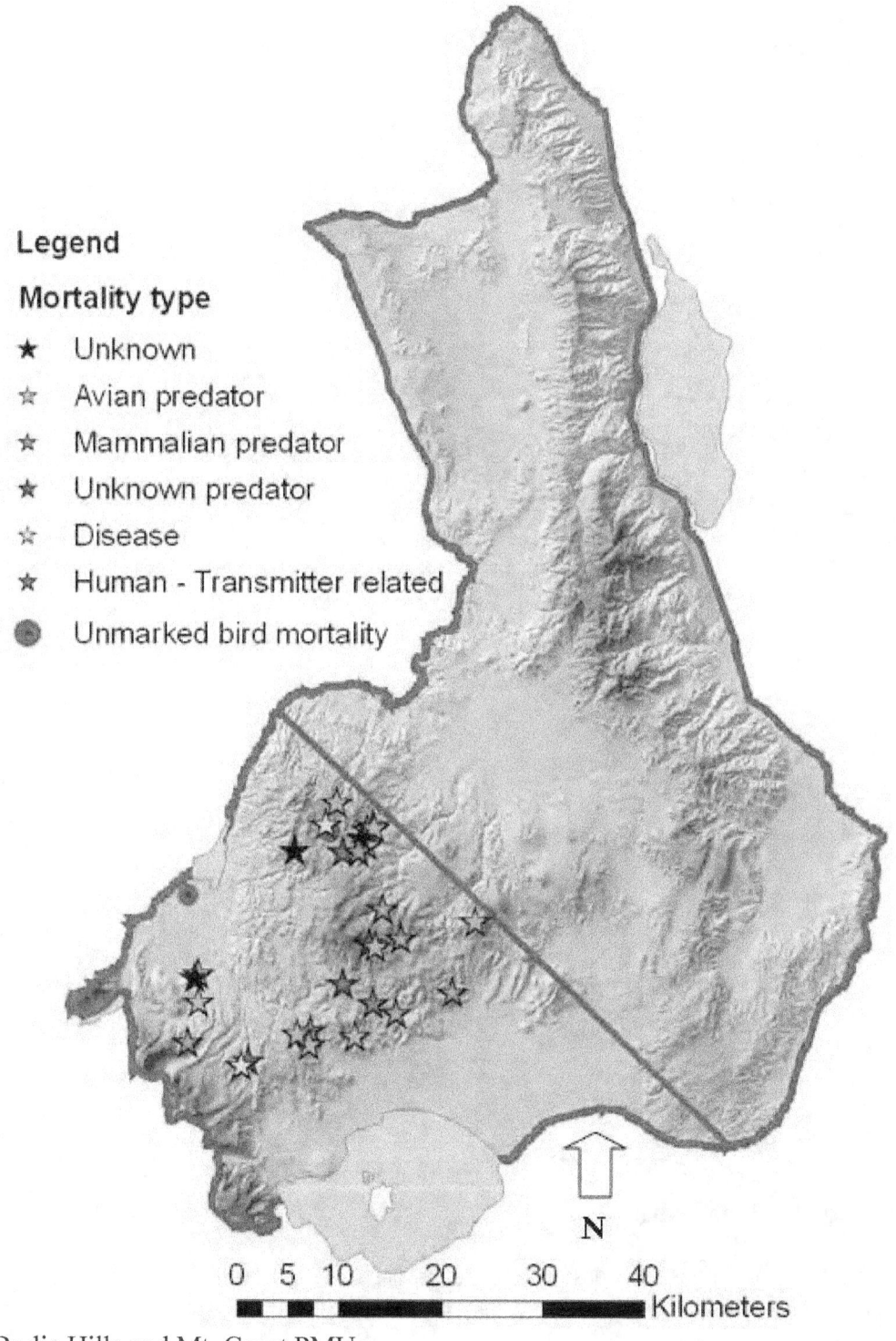

Legend

Mortality type

★ Unknown

☆ Avian predator

★ Mammalian predator

★ Unknown predator

☆ Disease

★ Human - Transmitter related

● Unmarked bird mortality

0 5 10   20   30   40

━━━━━━━━━━━━━━━━━━ Kilometers

N

Bodie Hills and Mt. Grant PMUs

Figure 17. Location and type of sage-grouse mortality event in the Bodie Hills PMU, 2003-2005.

Seasonal use areas encompassed a large proportion of the PMU and seemingly greater than seen in our other study areas (Figure 18). Mt. Grant PMU received use in both winters of 2003-04 and 2004-05, but use was more prevalent in 2004-05, while the Dry Lakes area was used less.

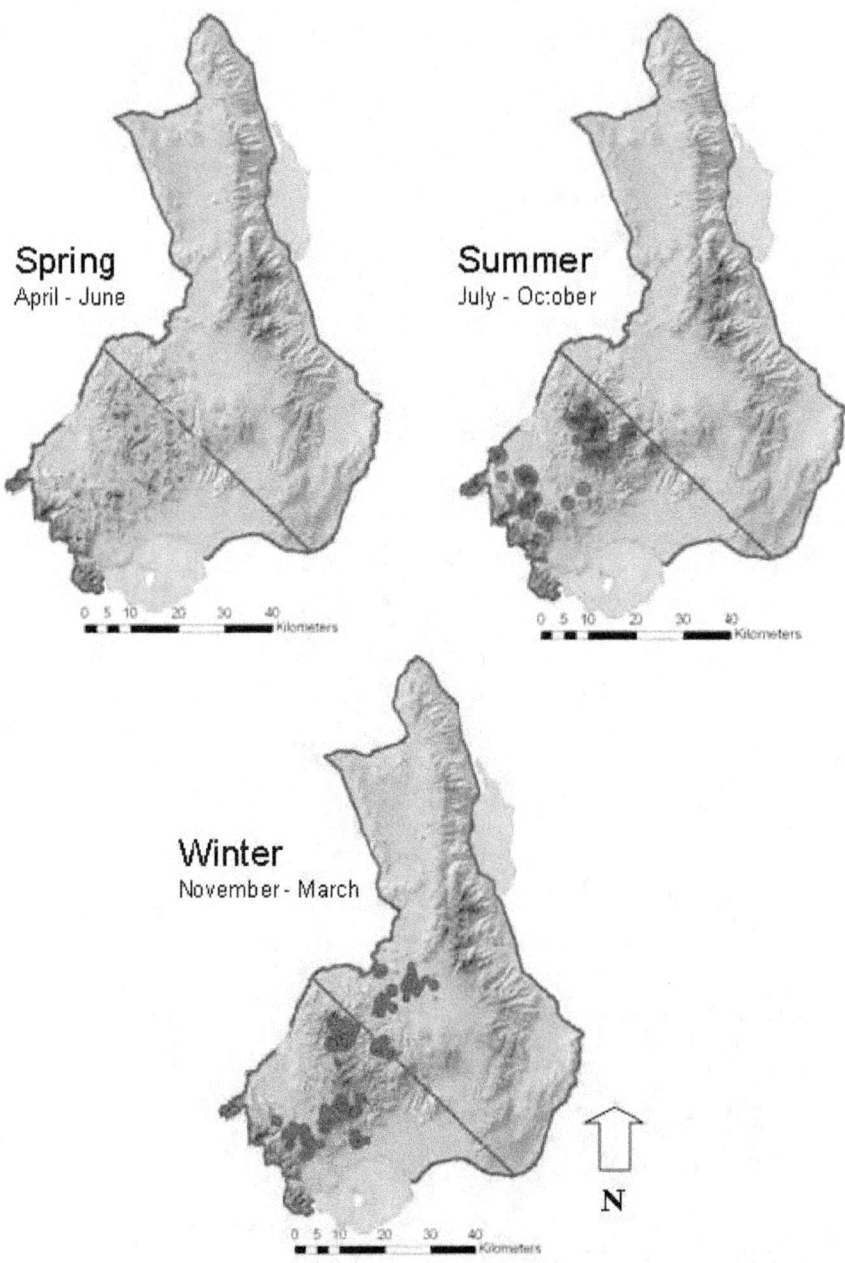

Bodie Hills and Mt. Grant PMUs

Figure 18. Seasonal sage-grouse use areas in the Bodie Hills and Mt. Grant PMUs 2003-2005. (Spring = April-June; Summer = July-October; Winter = November-March).

Land ownership within sage-grouse home ranges varied by season (Figure 19). Bureau of Land Management lands made up a large proportion of radio-marked sage-grouse homeranges, especially in the spring. Private lands were next in proportion of use and were most heavily used in the summer. Forest Service lands were proportionally most important in the winter and least important in the spring.

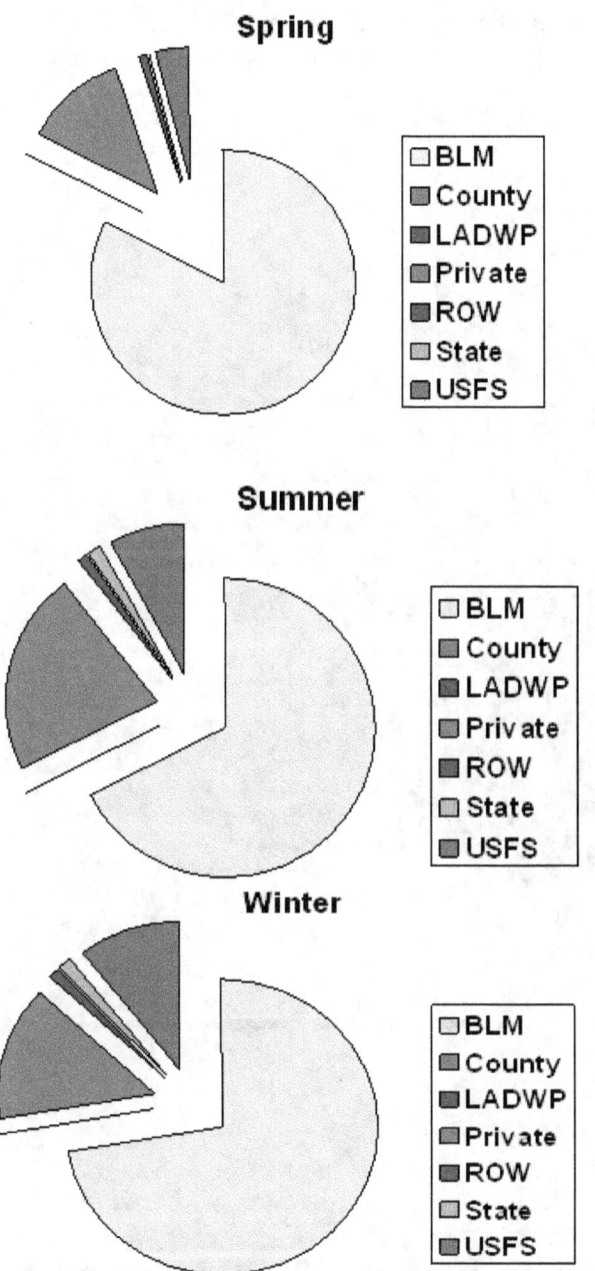

Figure 19. Land ownership of seasonal home ranges for radio-marked sage-grouse in the Bodie Hills and Mt. Grant PMUs, 2003-2005.

South Mono PMU

We tracked 48 sage-grouse (15 males, 33 females) in the South Mono PMU (Figure 20). Birds were trapped in Parker Meadows and at several locations in Long Valley. Spring captures were primarily at leks, fall captures occurred mostly on the edge of irrigated meadows that often serve as leks in the spring. Radio-marked grouse were tracked beginning the spring of 2003, and 16 transmitters remained active at the end of the study period in October 2005 (Table 2).

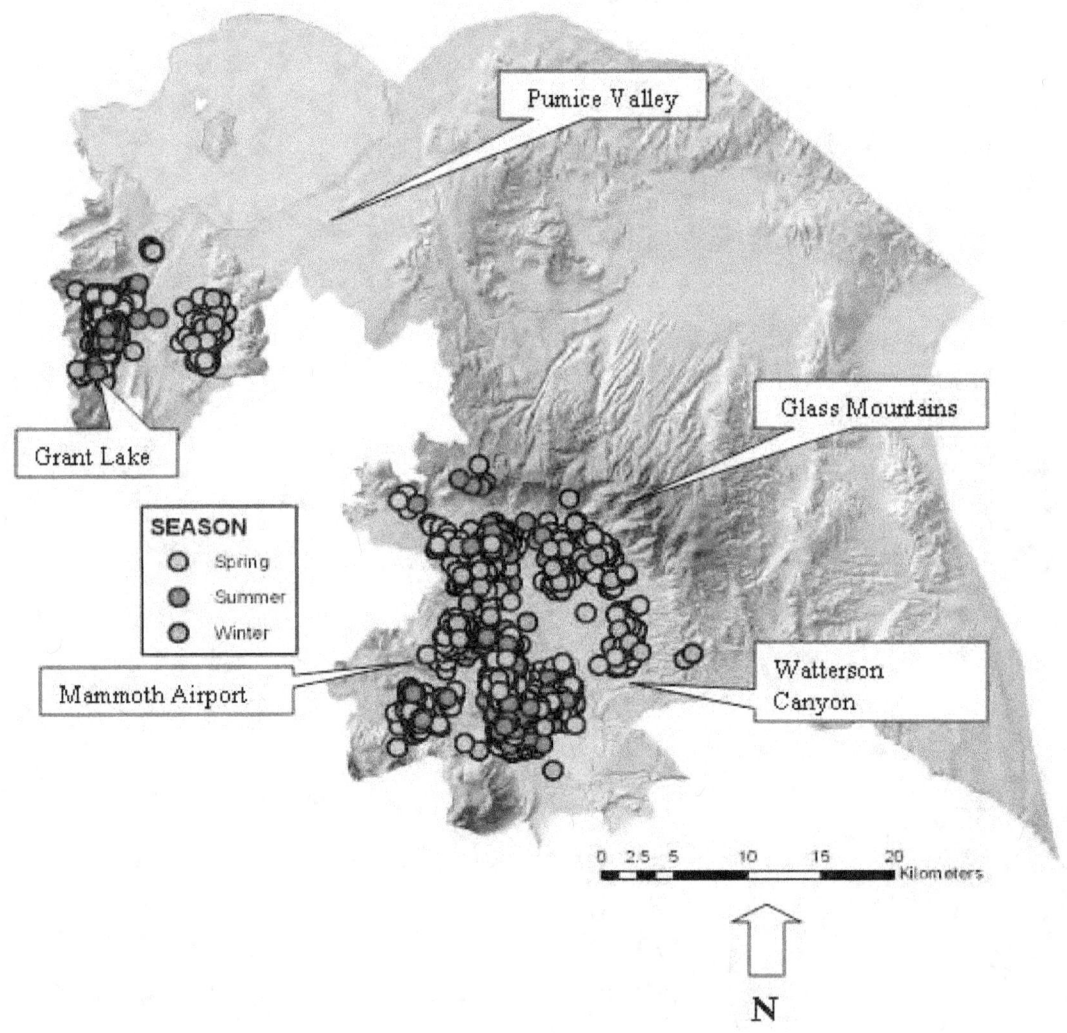

South Mono PMU

Figure 20. Radio-marked sage-grouse locations within the South Mono PMU, March 2003 – October 2005. (Spring = April-June; Summer = July-October; Winter = November-March).

We encountered large groups of unmarked sage-grouse on a regular basis throughout the Long Valley region (Figure 21). Groups of almost 300 were seen on the east side of Long Valley, especially during the winter period when much of the area was under deep snow.

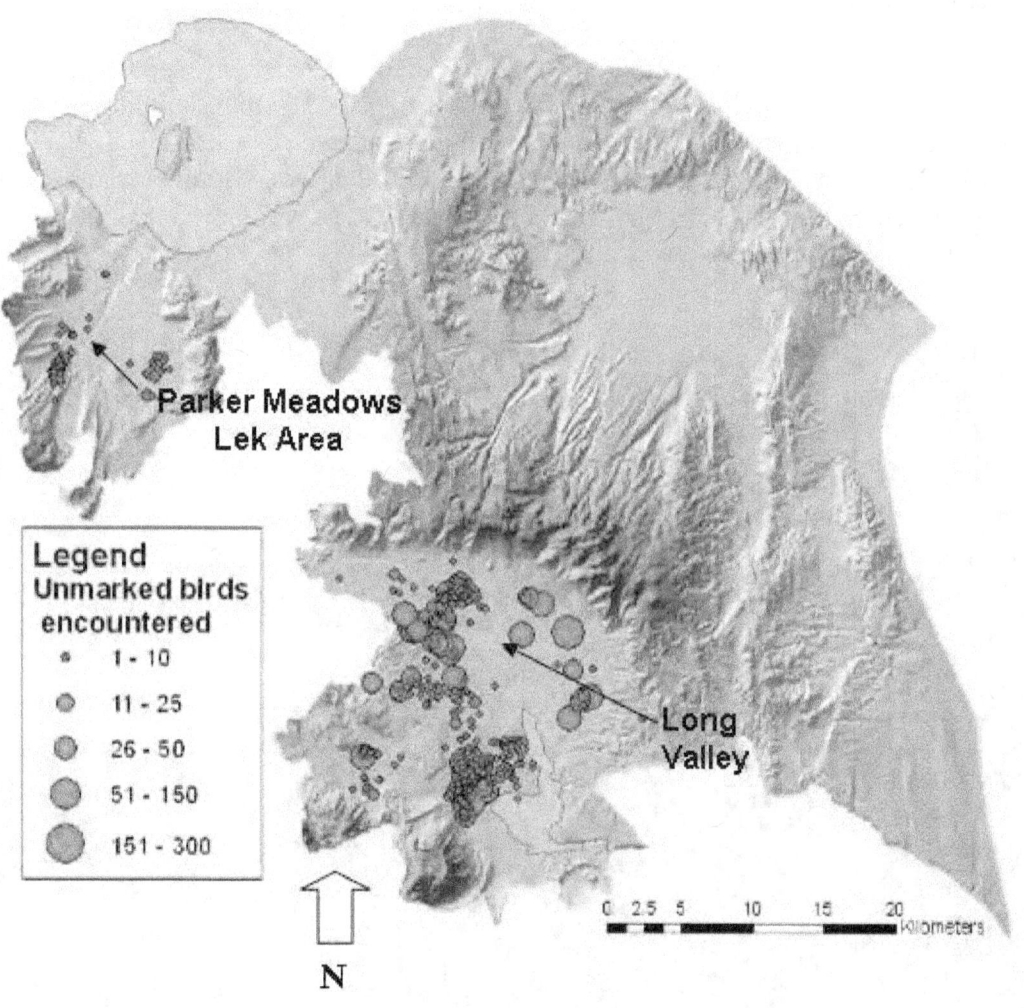

South Mono PMU

Figure 21. Location of unmarked sage-grouse observations obtained during field studies in the South Mono PMU, 2003-2005.

Nest placement by hens (Figure 22) in the South Mono PMU, coincided with spring home ranges. Most nests were near known leks, though several nests were far from any known active lek. In particular, one bird placed several nests at the base of the Glass Mountains, while two birds placed nests in southwest Long Valley. Of these, one had three nests within 1/3 mile of the Mammoth Airport, and the other had a nest near a historic lek at Laurel Pond.

The success of nests was very uneven in each area. All successful nests in Parker north of Sawmill Canyon, all on the moraine west of Grant Lake were unsuccessful (Figure 22). Within Long Valley all successful nests except two were near Benton Crossing Road from Whitmore Tubs to Little Alkali Lake and slopes west of Lek 4 (Figure 22). One of the remaining nests was at the base of the Glass Mountains and the brood survived only a few days after hatch. The remaining nest was between Hot Creek and Little Hot Creek, that brood survived one month.

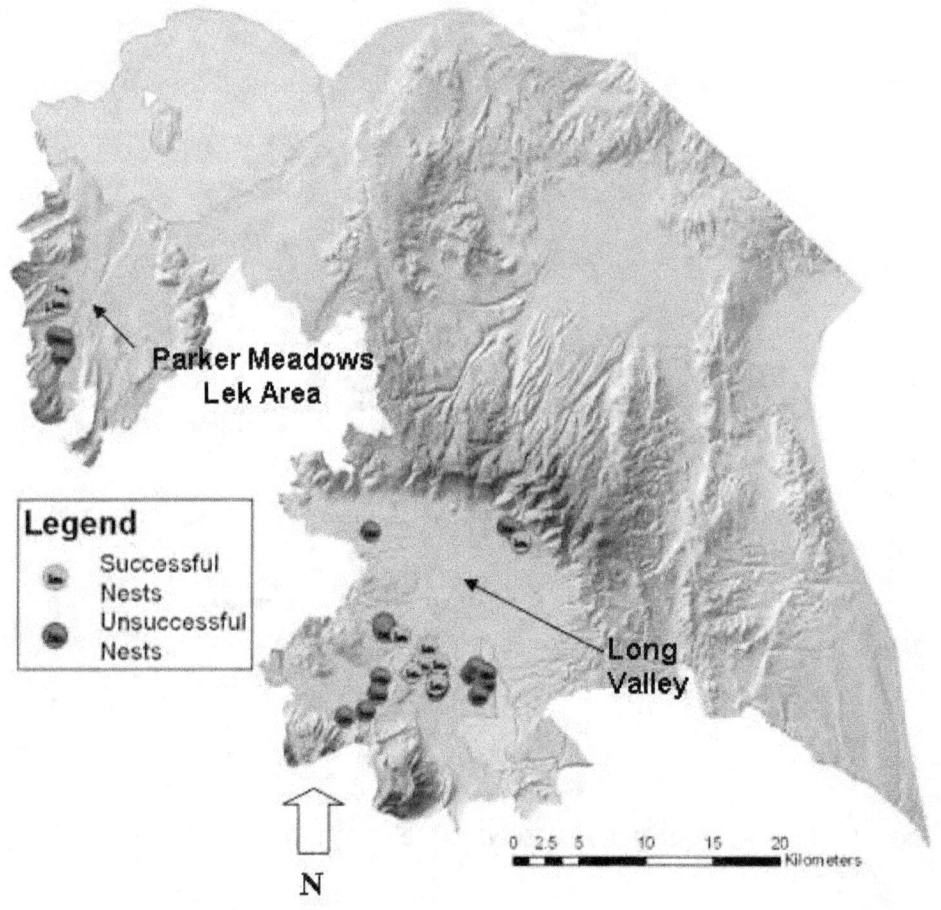

South Mono PMU

Figure 22. Nest locations of radio-marked sage-grouse in the South Mono PMU during the 2003-2005 nesting seasons.

Brood locations were often distributed around nest locations in dry and wet meadows (Figure 23). In Long Valley, main brood use areas included the Whitmore Tubs area extending to the hills over Little Alkali Lake and east of Benton Crossing Road from Whitmore Tubs to Lek 2 and Lek 3. In Parker Meadows, most brood locations were near the mouth of Sawmill Canyon and the meadow between Parker and Walker Creeks (Figure 23).

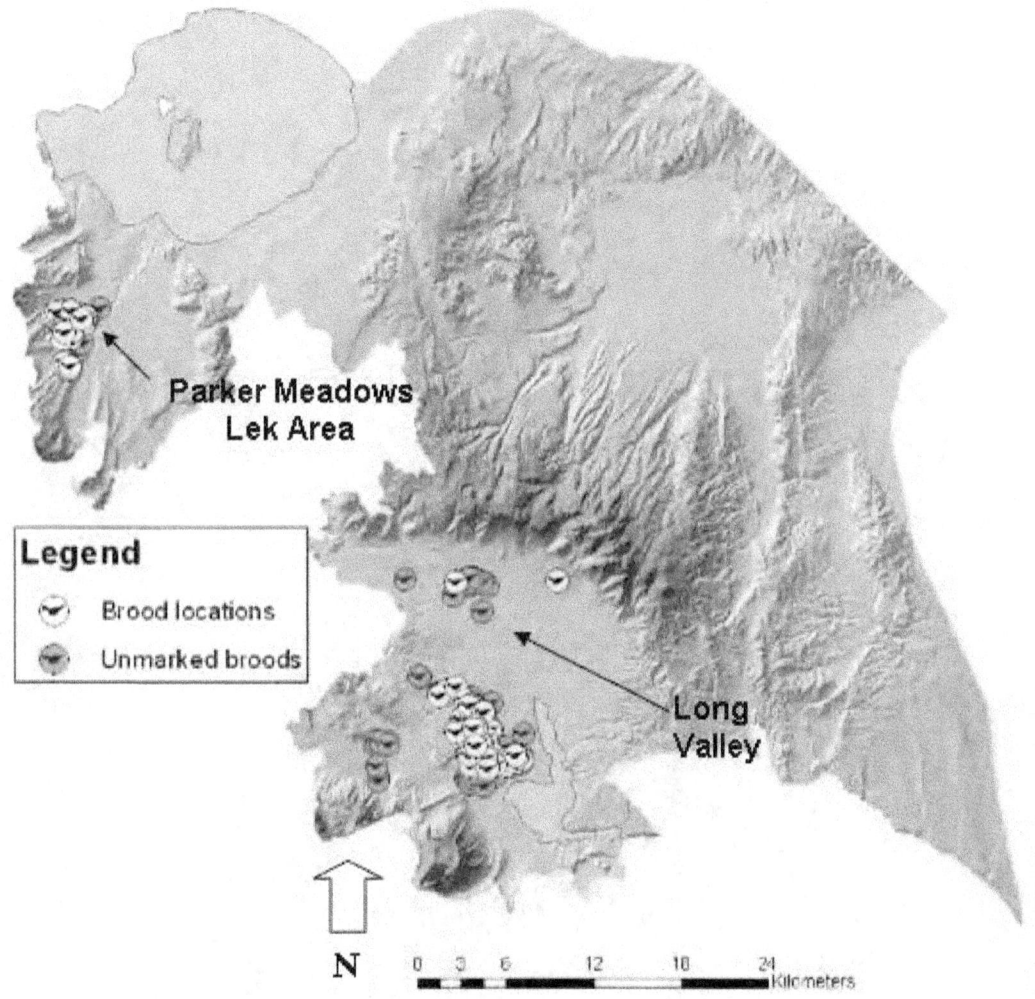

South Mono PMU

Figure 23. Locations of radio-marked sage-grouse hens with broods, and opportunistically encountered unmarked broods within the South Mono PMU, 2003-2005.

Sage-grouse in the Parker Meadows area had the most consistent home range, and overall the smallest home range of all areas studied (Table 3). Birds in Long Valley had very consistent spring and summer home ranges, but very different winter home ranges between years. We surmise that these differences are due to very different weather conditions between years. Year around use was very limited in Parker Meadows (Figure 20). Only the ridges west of Grant Lake had sufficient winter use to be considered occupied year-around.

The locations of mortality events were focused around the area of marking (i.e. near leks) in Long Valley (Figure 24). Most of the mortality events in the Long Valley area occurred in the summer and spring use areas while no mortalities occurred in the winter use areas east of Lake Crowley. Mortality events in the Parker Meadows area occurred in both winter and spring/summer habitat use areas. Unmarked bird mortality events were encountered frequently in the Long Valley area and most were in close proximity to radio-marked mortality events (Figure 24).

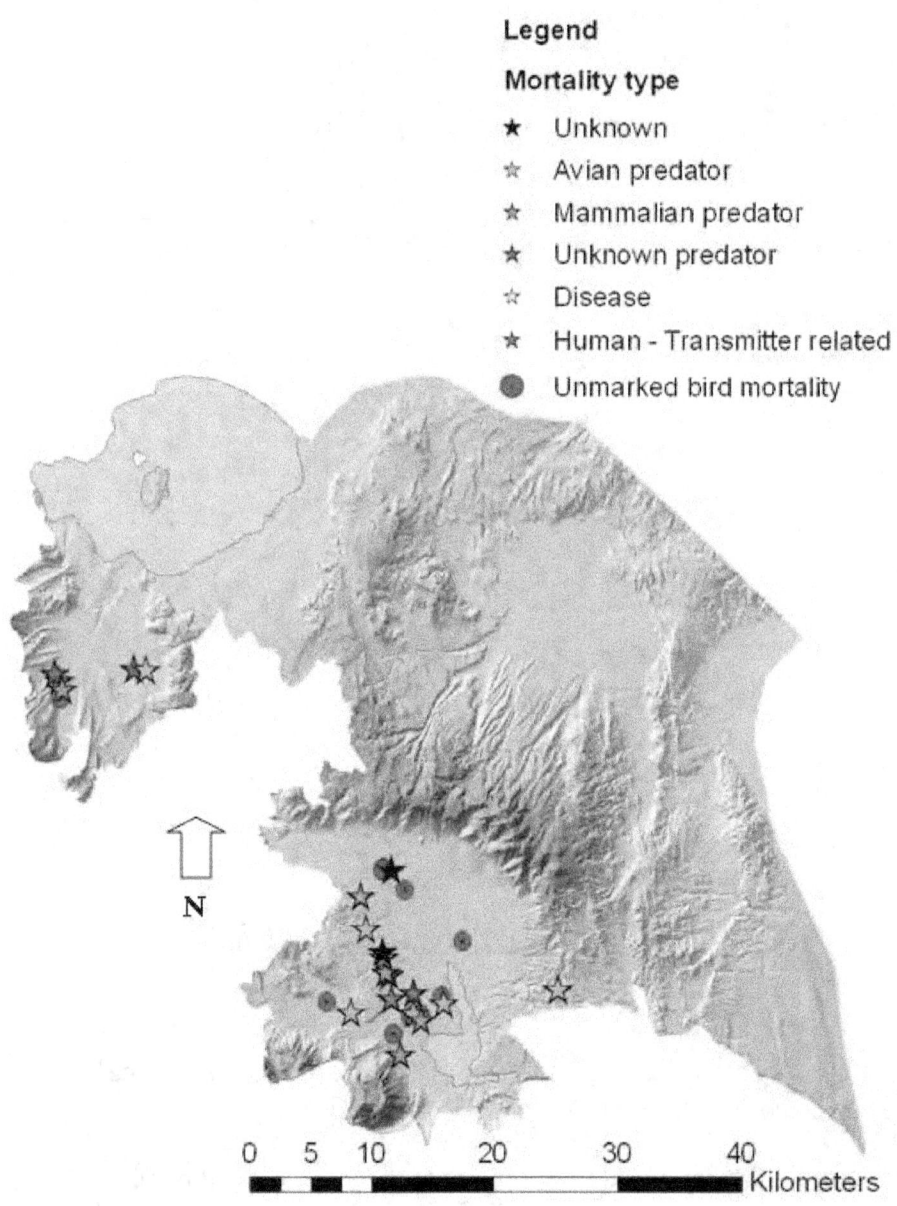

Legend

Mortality type

★ Unknown

☆ Avian predator

✦ Mammalian predator

✶ Unknown predator

✩ Disease

✻ Human - Transmitter related

● Unmarked bird mortality

0 5 10   20   30   40
Kilometers

South Mono PMU

Figure 24. Location and type of sage-grouse mortality events in the South Mono PMU, 2003-2005.

Spring and summer home ranges in Parker Meadows overlapped greatly (Figure 25). Meadows along Parker Creek and the slopes north of Sawmill canyon were used heavily during spring and summer in all years. Winter and some early spring locations occurred on the east side of Pumice Valley, north of the Aeolian Buttes. Use of this area appeared to relate to snow depth, as birds would often move back to the west side of Hwy-395 after extended warm periods. Year around use in Long Valley included a large area between Lake Crowley on the south and east, Alkali Flat on the north, and between Hot Creek and Little Hot Creek on the west (Figure 20). Sage-grouse also used a small area north of the airport during all seasons, though expanded use south and west of the airport was evident in the spring and summer.

During the spring, sage-grouse used several areas along the Owens River north and west of Benton Crossing Road and an area northeast of Lake Crowley near Waterson Canyon (Figure 25). Heavy summer use of meadows along the Owens River near the high voltage power line occurred in all years. Winter home range patterns in Long Valley were very divergent between periods of low snowfall and high snowfall. During the relatively low snowfall winter of 2003-2004, sage-grouse stayed near a bench north of Little Hot Creek on the west side of Long Valley and between Benton Crossing Road and O'Harrel Canyon on the north side. Similar patterns were evident early in the winter of 2004-2005, but following heavy storms during the last weeks of 2004, almost every bird moved to the east side of Long Valley from Watterson Troughs Road north to Wilfred Creek and along the base of the Glass Mountains west to O'Harrel Canyon. These areas have some of the tallest sage (Mountain, Basin, and Wyoming big sagebrush) in Long Valley. Birds that remained in wintering areas from 2003-2004 were observed digging through several inches of snow to reach the top of sagebrush plants in those areas.

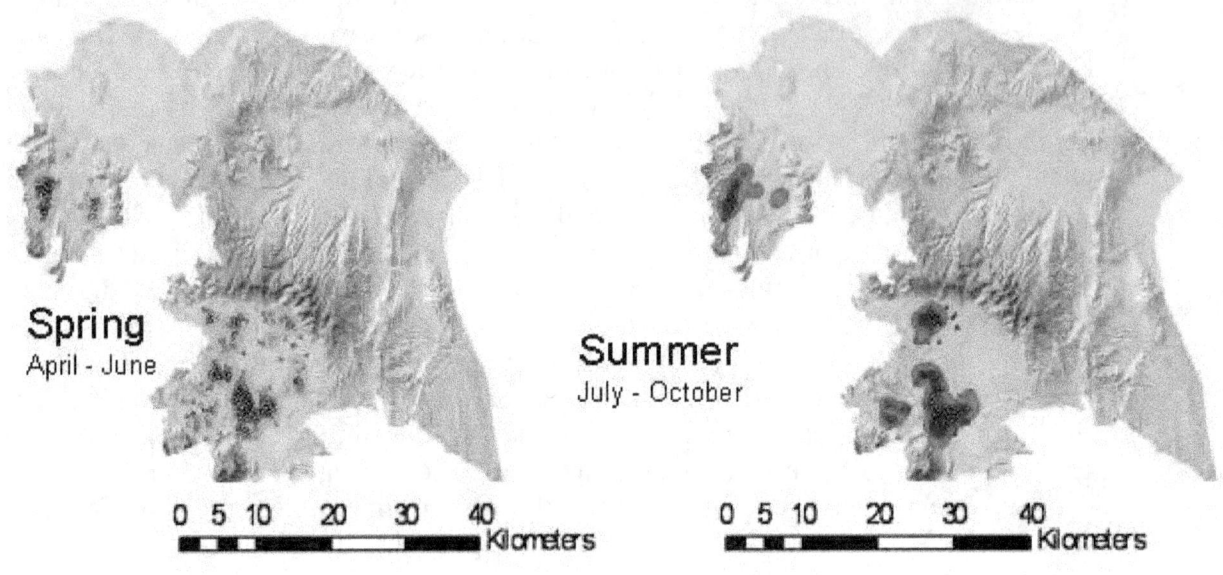

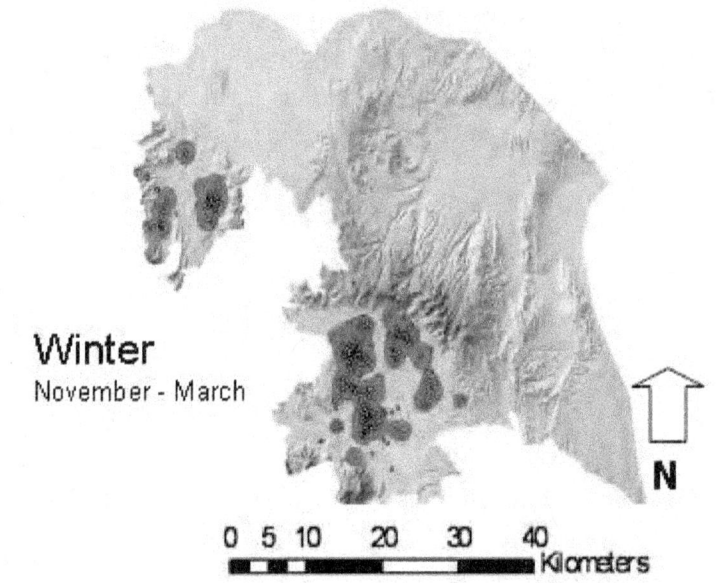

South Mono PMU

Figure 25. Seasonal sage-grouse use areas within the South Mono PMU, 2003-2005.

Land ownership in the South Mono PMU was more diverse (Figure 26) than the other areas (Figure 4). The largest proportion of spring and winter home ranges was USFS land. Summer home ranges occurred predominantly on LADWP land. Radio-marked grouse used private lands and BLM administered lands similarly across seasons.

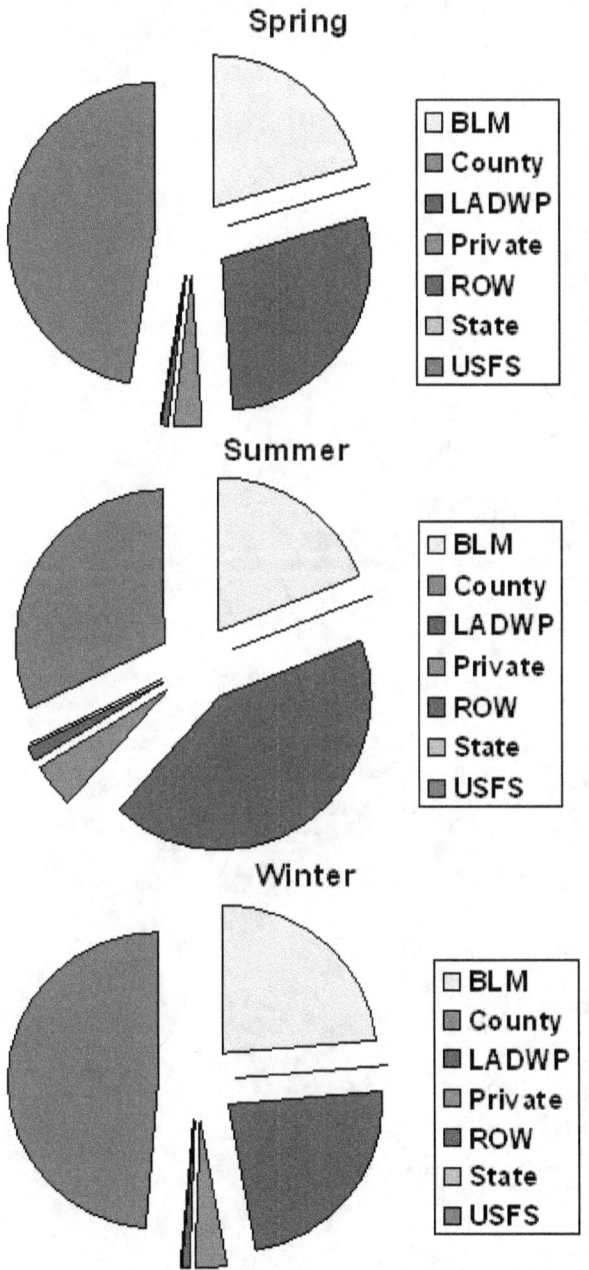

Figure 26. Land ownership within seasonal home ranges for radio-marked sage-grouse in the South Mono PMU, 2003-2005.

White Mountains PMU

We trapped and radio-marked 25 individual sage-grouse (7 males and 18 females) at Red Peak, Sage Hen Peak, Cottonwood, and Crooked Creek drainages within the California portion of the White Mountains population management unit (Table 1). We obtained ground telemetry locations for radio-marked birds during late spring and summer in 2004 and 2005 (Figure 27).

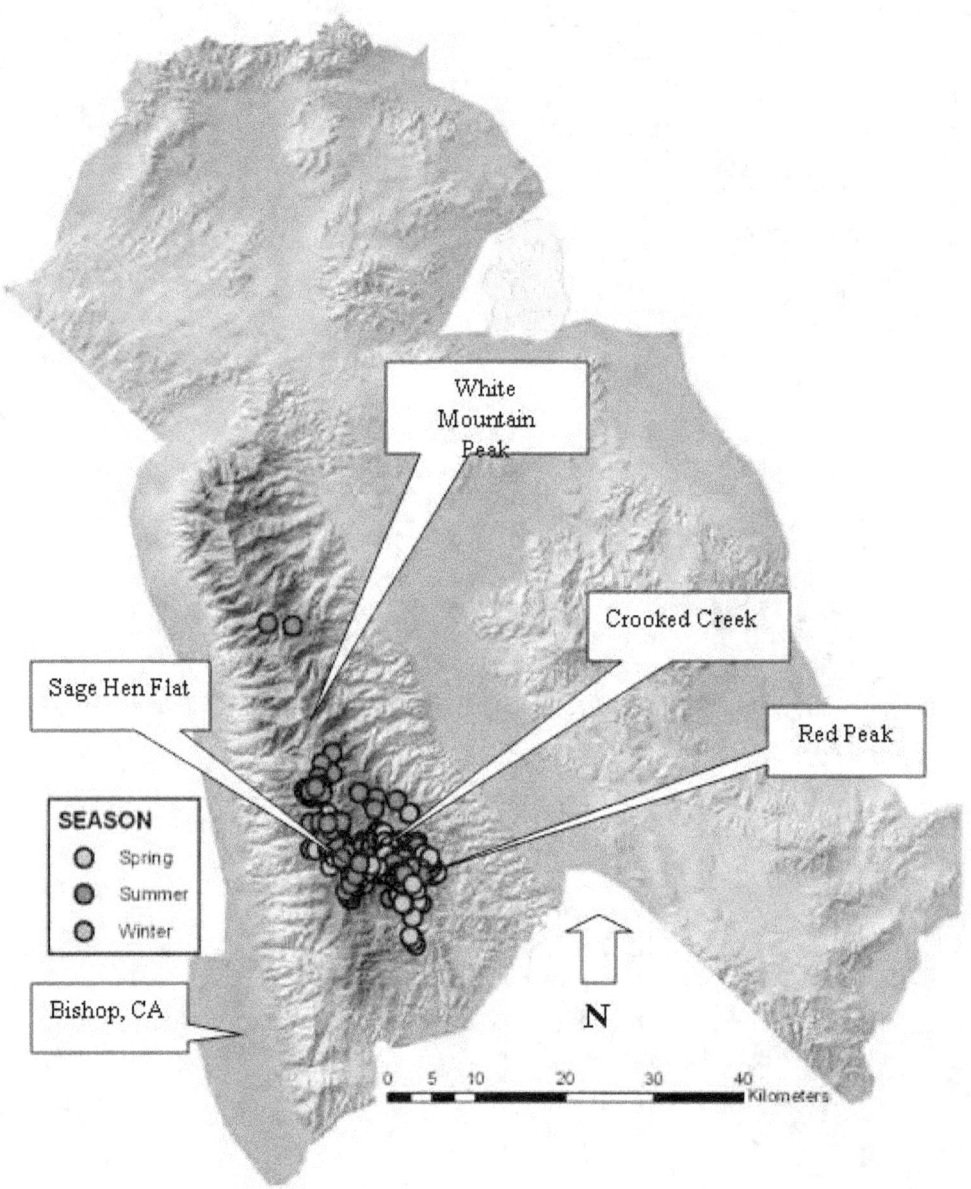

White Mountains PMU

Figure 27. Radio-marked sage-grouse locations within the White Mountains PMU, March 2003-October 2005. (Spring = April-June; Summer = July-October; Winter = November-March).

Winter and early spring locations were obtained through aerial telemetry. Locations recorded for unmarked birds were in similar locations as marked bird locations (Figure 28).

Nest locations and brood identification were not easily obtainable either year, due to weather and snow conditions. Aerial telemetry during the winter seasons illustrated potential migration away from spring and summer areas, but was not sufficient to characterize winter distribution and movements of sage-grouse from the study area. We recommend caution when interpreting winter home ranges as they illustrate only a portion of the winter range of these birds. Evaluation of winter movements and distribution of birds in this PMU will require further examination, possibly using GPS or satellite transmitter technology.

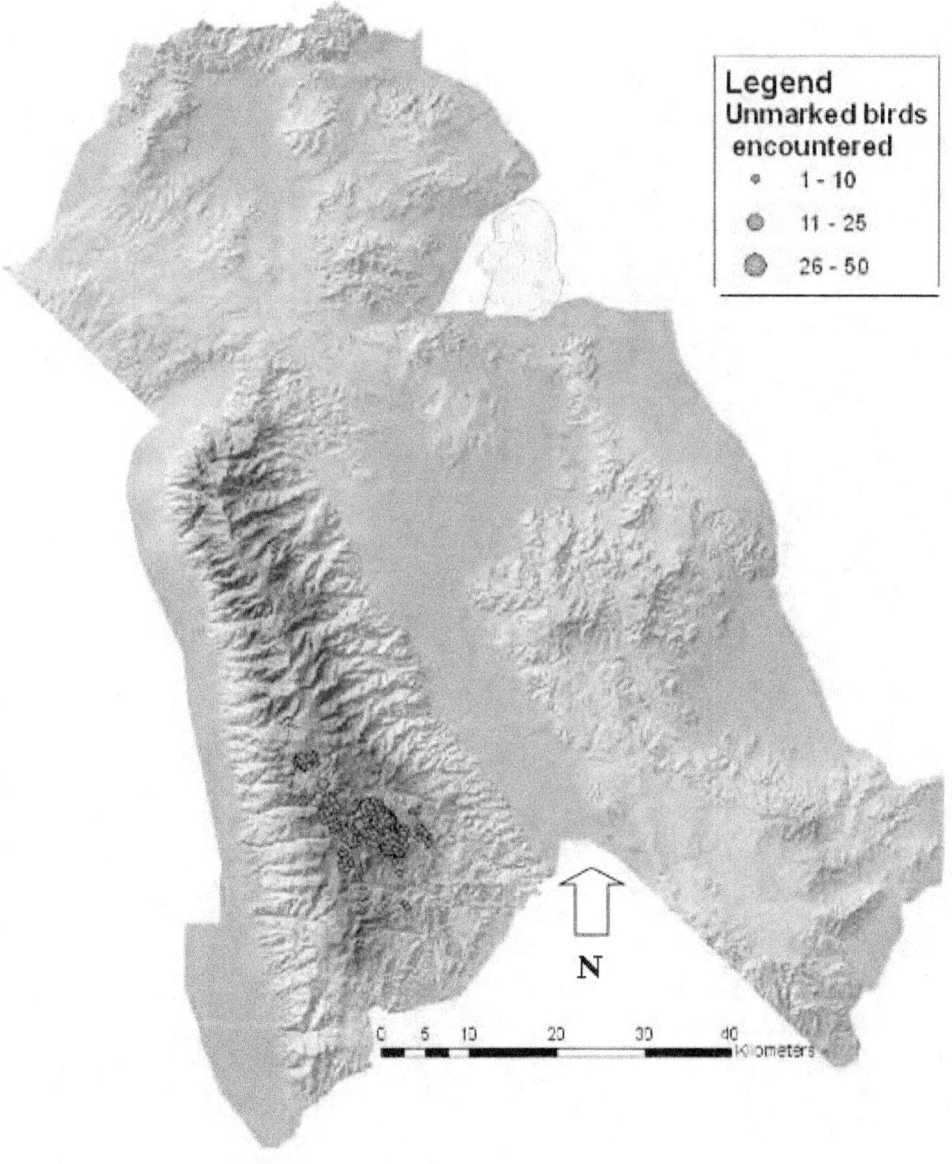

Figure 28. Location of unmarked sage-grouse observations obtained during field studies in the White Mountains PMU, 2003-2005.

Many grouse had already begun nesting by the time the study area was accessible each spring. We discovered only one nest in each year during the study (Figure 29). However, all hens located between March and June occupied somewhat restricted areas west of County Line Hill, suggesting a similarly restricted nesting area. The 2004 nest was located high on the ridge south of Station Peak, west of Iron Mountain and north of Sage Hen Peak (Figure 29). The flat between Sage Hen Peak and Iron Mountain is the location of a lek discovered by USGS and CDFG personnel in 2004. The 2005 nest located near the ridge top of the Upper North Fork Crooked Creek drainage belonged to an unmarked hen. Brood rearing areas included ridge tops near the 2004 nest and North and South Fork Crooked Creek drainage bottoms (Figure 30).

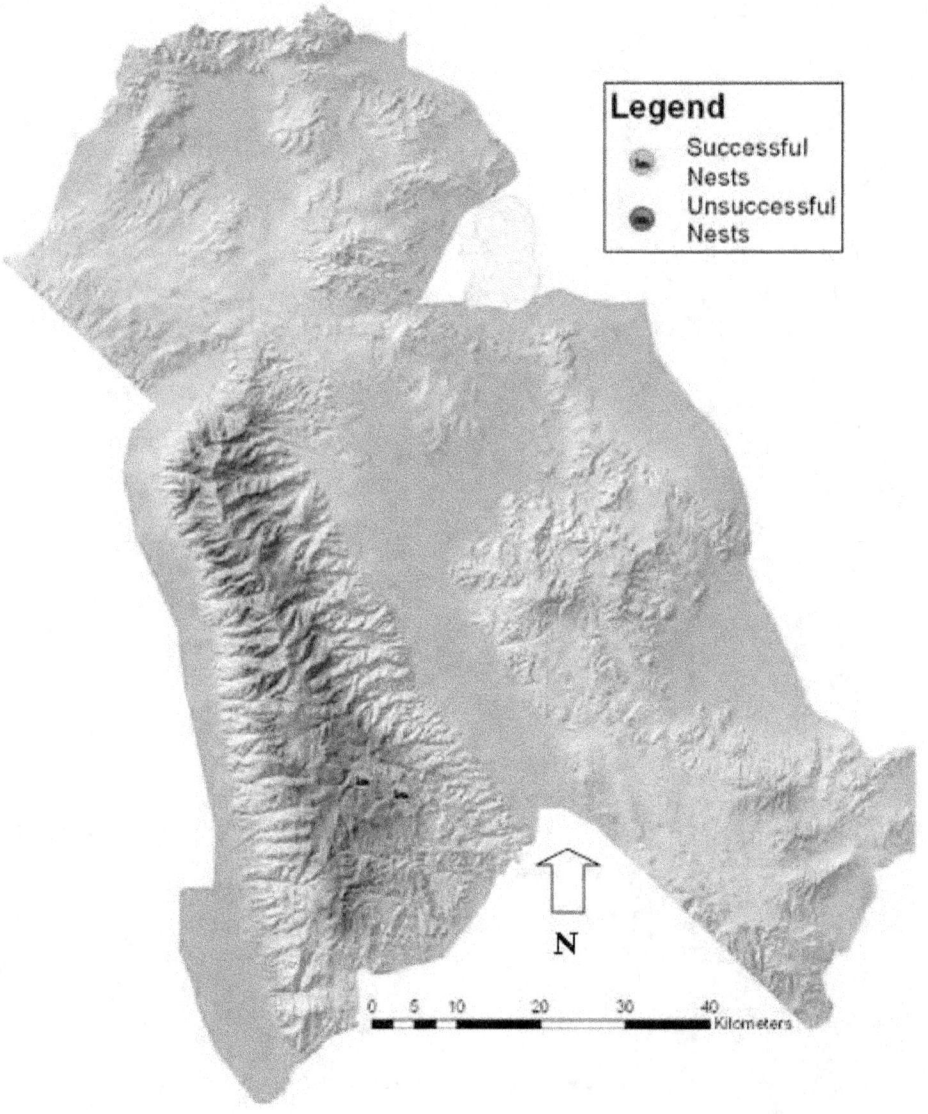

White Mountain PMU

Figure 29. Radio-marked sage-grouse nest locations within the White Mountains PMU, 2003-2005.

Brood locations from radio-marked hens are limited due to the low number of nests discovered (Figure 29). The radio-marked hen with the nest that was discovered in 2004 remained in the vicinity of Station Peak for several weeks before moving to the confluence of North and South Forks of Crooked Creek. Radio-marked hens with broods were also seen along Crooked Creek Sage Hen Peak and north of Sage Hen Flat. We found one radio-marked hen with a brood on Robert's Ridge in 2005 before they moved to Red Peak. We found unmarked hens with broods in additional areas, including Sage Hen Flat, the headwaters of Mill Canyon, Campito Mountain, and County Line Hill (Figure 30). Multiple brood sightings also occurred in a drainage on the south slope of Mount Barcroft.

Birds utilized the Crooked Creek drainage between Red Peak and Bucks Peak, Station Peak, and North Fork Crooked Creek drainage throughout the year (Figure 27). We were unable to calculate annual home range for the White Mountain due to sample size limitations.

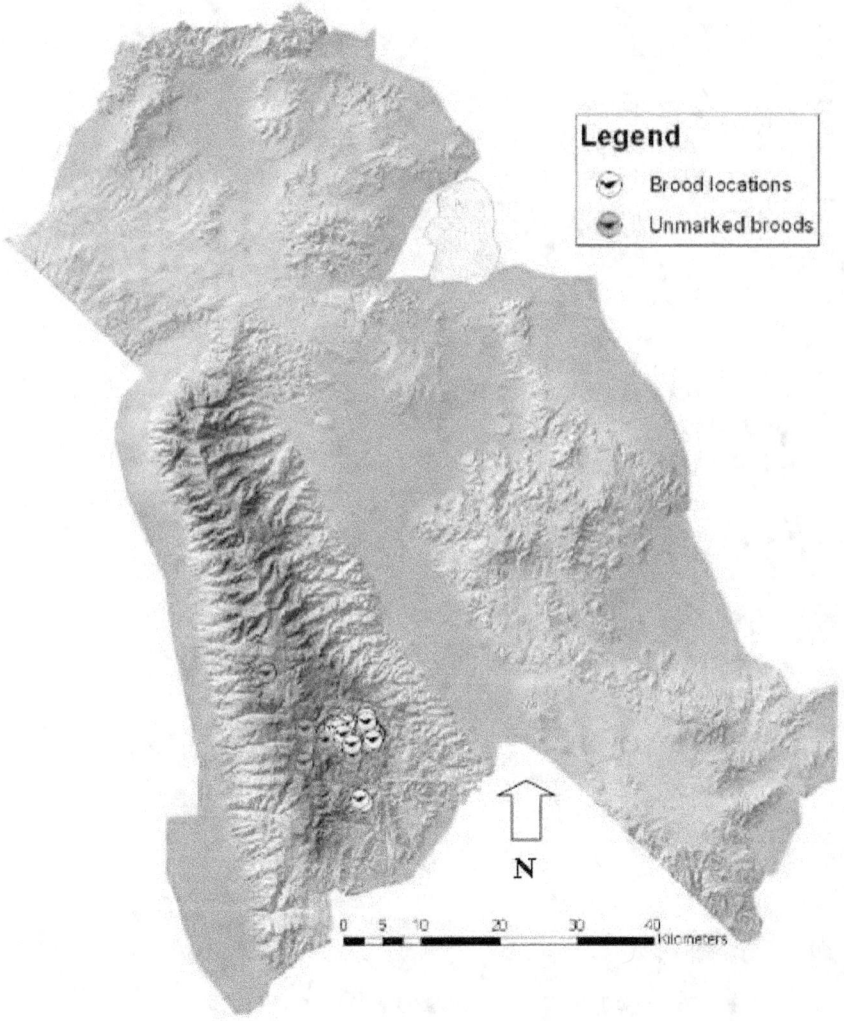

White Mountains PMU

Figure 30. Locations of radio-marked sage-grouse hens with broods, and opportunistically encountered unmarked broods within the White Mountains PMU 2003-2005.

Mortality events for radio-marked birds were concentrated near core use areas (Figure 31). Avian predation was the primary cause of mortality in this area, although sample size limits the interpretation of these results (Table 4).

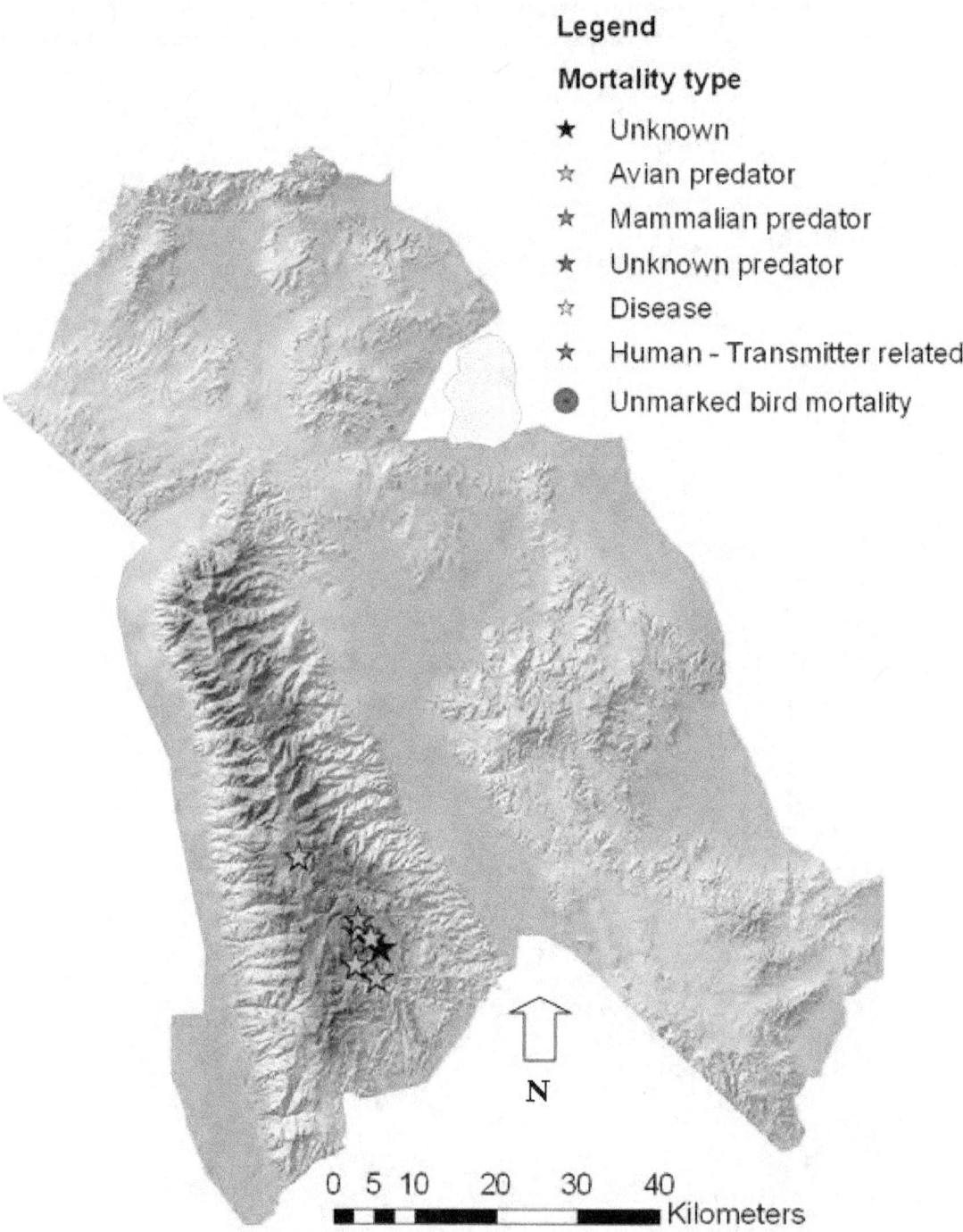

Figure 31. Location and type of sage-grouse mortality event in the White Mountains PMU, 2003-2005.

Identified wintering areas included the higher elevations in this region and in Tres Plumas Flat and the headwaters of Mill Canyon (Figure 32). During spring and summer birds used Campito Meadow and Sheep Mountain to the north and Campito Mountain to the south and County Line Hill. Sage-grouse also occupied the upper portions of the North Fork Crooked Creek Drainage, along the road to Cottonwood Creek, and the South Fork Crooked Creek during spring and summer (Figure 32). Spring use areas included Sage Hen Peak and Robert's Ridge (Figure 32). Summer use occurred at Sage Hen Flat and the area between Mount Barcroft and Piute Mountain. Isolated summer locations recorded west of Mount Barcroft in the McAfee Meadows and on Tres Plumas Flat indicate connectivity despite intervening forest. A single male found during a telemetry flight on Chiatovich Flat in mid July and again early August subsequently moved back to the Crooked Creek drainage (Figure 32). Lack of winter and spring locations despite ground and aerial tracking suggests an unknown connected pocket of habitat and possibly interconnected populations with grouse near Trail Canyon or the South Mono PMU.

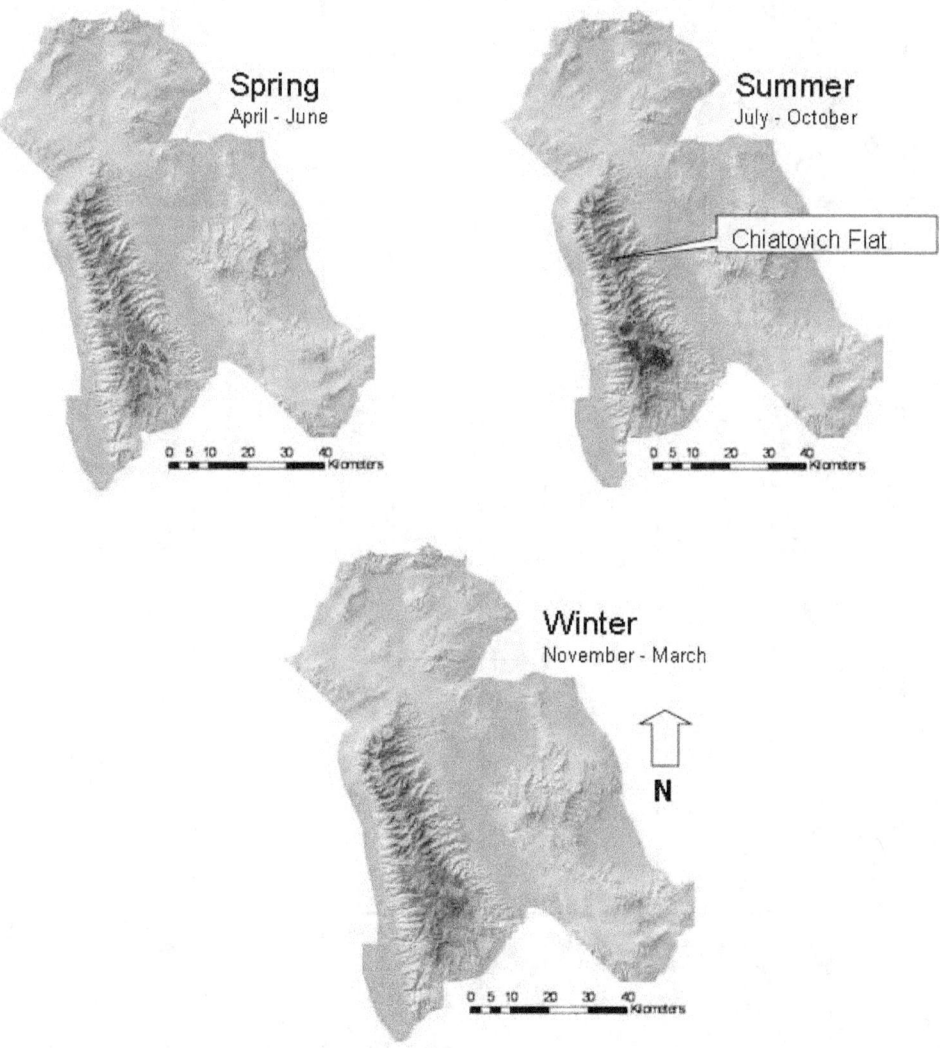

Figure 32. Seasonal sage-grouse use areas within the White Mountains PMU (Spring = April-June; Summer = July-October; Winter = November-March).

41

Table 1. Number of sage-grouse radio-marked during each season within all study areas. Spring captures occurred March-June, Fall captures occurred September-December.

PMU Study Site	2003 Spring Female	2003 Spring Male	2003 Fall Female	2003 Fall Male	2004 Spring Female	2004 Spring Male	2004 Fall Female	2004 Fall Male	2005 Spring Female	2005 Spring Male	Total
Desert Creek-Fales											
Jackass	10	2			4	2					18
Fales†	7	2			4	4					17
Total	17	4			8	6					35
Bodie Hills	6	4	14	3			6	2	2		37
South Mono											
Parker	4	2			4	1					11
Long Valley	10	3	5	5	2	3			8	1	37
Total	14	5	5	5	6	4			8	1	48
White Mountains			5		2	5	11	2			25
Grand Total	37	13	24	8	16	15	17	4	10	1	145

† - The Fales study area includes birds captured at both Burcham and Wheeler Flats.

Table 2. Transmitters still active at midpoint of Spring and Fall/Winter seasons. Birds captured after May 1 or Nov. 1 are not represented in that season's active transmitters.

PMU / Study Site	Active May 1, 2003		Active Nov. 1, 2003		Active May 1, 2004		Active Nov. 1, 2004		Active May 1, 2005		Active at end of study period (October 2005)	
	Female	Male	Female	Male	Female	Male	Female	Male	Female	Male	Female	Male
Desert Creek-Fales												
Jackass	9	1	5		9	2	8		8		4	
Fales†	6	2	1		5	2	2	1	1			
Total	15	3	6		14	4	10	1	9		4	
Bodie Hills	5	3	1	2	14	3	15	4	11	3	5	1
South Mono												
Parker	3	1	2	2	5	2	4	2	4	1	2	1
Long Valley	7	3	14	5	12	4	10	4	15	3	12	1
Total	10	4	16	7	17	6	14	6	19	4	14	2
White Mountains			5		6	5	9	7	8	5	5	5
Grand Total	30	10	28	9	51	18	48	18	47	12	28	8

† - The Fales study area includes birds captured at both Burcham and Wheeler Flats.

Table 3. Mean annual home range sizes for radio-marked sage-grouse by capture site, year and sex. Home ranges were calculated for each bird having at least 30 telemetry locations and at least 5 points in each of three seasons (Spring = April-June; Summer = July – October; Winter = November – March) using the 95% fixed kernel method.

Capture Site	N	Sex	Year	Mean Annual Home Range (ha)	Smallest Home Range (ha)	Largest Home Range (ha)
Jackass	5	F	03-04	1,334	263	3,597
Jackass	4	F	04-05	5,740	3,263	10,443
Fales	1	F	03-04	1,741	1,741	1,741
Fales	1	F	04-05	3,447	3,447	3,447
Fales	1	M	04-05	608	608	608
Bodie Hills	1	F	03-04	9,096	9,096	9,096
Bodie Hills	5	F	04-05	7,585	2,601	13,814
Bodie Hills	2	M	03-04	20,936	17,071	24,801
Parker	2	F	03-04	1,352	723	1,981
Parker	2	F	04-05	1,676	1,260	2,091
Parker	2	M	03-04	2,230	2,144	2,315
Parker	1	M	04-05	1,173	1,173	1,173
Long Valley	9	F	03-04	3,473	1,010	4,994
Long Valley	4	F	04-05	2,996	1,548	4,128
Long Valley	3	M	04-05	3,643	2,485	4,954

Table 4. Causes of mortality for radio-marked sage-grouse recorded by population management unit (PMU).

PMU	Avian predator	Mammalian predator	Unknown predator	Unknown	Handling Related	West Nile Virus
Desert Creek/Fales	6	7	8	7	0	1
Bodie Hills	11	6	5	2	2	3
South Mono	6	11	4	2	2	0
White Mountains	6	2	1	1	0	0
Total	29	26	18	12	4	4

Table 5. Nesting summary for all nests from radio-marked sage-grouse within the Bi-State Planning Area 2003-2005. Censored nests include instances where identification of the nesting site may have influenced nest fate. Nest predator identification for 2003, 2004, and two-thirds of 2005 nests determined from remains at nest site. Remaining 2005 nests determined from infrared video cameras (3 mammal and 2 avian predators).

Season	Number of Initial Nests	Renests	# successful	# unsuccessful			Average clutch size	Nest initiation rate[†]	# censored
2003	20	2	11	11			6.55	84.0%	8
				10	1	0			
2004	36	5	23	18			6.31	86.4%	3
				14	3	1			
2005	28	4	19	13			6.70	71.4%	4
				7	5	1			
				Mammal predation	Avian predation	Abandoned			

† - Nest initiation rate is the nominal rate observed. Actual rate of initiation may be higher than reported, especially in 2005 when weather prevented access to birds in remote, high elevation study areas.

Table 6. Nominal annual reproductive success of radio-marked birds (proportion of sage-grouse hens hatching ≥1 egg) between 2003 and 2005 for all study areas.

Study Area	# hens during all breeding seasons	# successful nests	Annual reproductive success
Bodie Hills	30	18	60.0%
Fales	9	4	44.4%
Jackass Flat	24	14	58.3%
Parker	9[†]	6	66.7%
Long Valley	32	11	34.4%
Total	104	53	51.0%

† - Three hens removed due to problems with transmitter fit.

Table 7. Transect shrub cover and sagebrush (Artemisia sp.) height at sage-grouse nest sites and adjacent random locations in the Bi-State Planning Area excluding White Mountains PMU.

Study area[†]	Nests	DR[‡] Points	IR[‡] Points	Nest % Shrub Cover	DR % Shrub Cover	IR % Shrub Cover	Nest Sage Height (cm)	DR Sage Height (cm)	IR Sage Height (cm)
BH	27	27	23	54.47	50.72	42.70	53.34	40.50	50.35
JA	22	21	14	45.67	37.42	34.76	43.09	40.78	38.73
LV	37	40	41	46.44	43.70	35.34	59.79	51.63	67.22
PA	11	9	9	53.49	51.51	44.69	54.97	52.31	51.98
FA	10	10	11	56.80	42.16	43.27	64.11	58.46	50.26

† BH = Bodie Hills, JA = Jackass Flat, LV = Long Valley, PA = Parker Meadows, FA = Fales Hot spring

‡ DR – Dependent Random points located 50-200m from the nest, IR – Independent Random points located within the study area

References Cited

Bi-State Sage-grouse Conservation Team. 2004. Greater sage-grouse conservation plan for Nevada and eastern California. First edition – June 30, 2004. URL: *http://www.ndow.org/wild/sg/plan/SGPlan063004.pdf*

Connelly, J. W., M. A. Schroeder, A. R. Sands, and C. E. Braun. 2000. Guidelines to manage sage-grouse populations and their habitats. Wildlife Society Bulletin. 28:967-985.

Connelly, J. W., S. T. Knick, M. A. Schroeder, and S. J. Stiver. 2004. Conservation assessment of greater sage-grouse and sagebrush habitats. Western Association of Fish and Wildlife Agencies. Unpublished Report. Cheyenne, Wyoming.

Deibert, P. A., 2005. Status Review Completed: Greater Sage-Grouse Not Warranted for Listing as Endangered or Threatened. US Fish and Wildlife Service News Release – January 7, 2005. Washington D.C.

Giesen, K.M., T. J. Schoenberg, and C.E. Braun. 1982. Methods for trapping Sage-grouse in Colorado. Wildlife Society Bulletin. 10:224-231.

Oyler-McCance, S. J., S. E. Taylor, and T. W. Quinn. 2005. A multilocus population genetic survey of the greater sage-grouse across their range. Molecular Ecology. 14:1293-1310.

Riley, T.Z., and B.A. Fistler. 1992. Necklace radio transmitter attachment for pheasants. Journal of the Iowa Academy of Science. 99(2-3):65-66.

Sveum, C.M., J.A. Crawford, and W.D. Edge. 1998. Use and selection of brood-rearing habitat by sage-grouse in south central Washington. Great Basin Naturalist. 58(4):344-351.

Wakkinen, W. L., K. P. Reese, J. W. Connelly, and R. A. Fischer. 1992. An improved spotlighting technique for capturing sage-grouse. Wildlife Society Bulletin. 20:425-426.